D. STUART BRISCOE

PLAYING BY THE RULES

BY D. Stuart Briscoe:
Spirit Life
God's Way to Live Successfully
Playing by the Rules

D. STUART BRISCOE

PLAYING
—BY THE—
RULES

Fleming H. Revell Company
Old Tappan, New Jersey

Unless otherwise identified Scripture quotations are taken from the HOLY BIBLE: NEW INTERNATIONAL VERSION. Copyright © 1973, 1978 by the International Bible Society. Used by permission of Zondervan Bible Publishers.

Scripture quotations identified KJV are from the King James Version of the Bible.

Quotation from *What Works When Life Doesn't,* by Stuart Briscoe, used by permission of Victor Books.

Library of Congress Cataloging in Publication Data

Briscoe, D. Stuart.
  Playing by the rules.

  Bibliography: p.
  1. Ten commandments. I. Title.
BV4655.B68 1986   241.5′2   86-13938
ISBN 0-8007-1489-X

Copyright © 1986 by D. Stuart Briscoe
Published by the Fleming H. Revell Company
Old Tappan, New Jersey 07675
Printed in the United States of America

Contents

Preface

Another book on the Ten Commandments?

Yes, and I'll tell you why! As I read a number of serious books on the subject, I found that most of them addressed issues of concern and interest in the day they were published, but often said little or nothing about the issues we confront today. For instance one writer seemed desperately concerned about Sabbath keeping, but said nothing about abortion or nuclear war—for the obvious reason that they were not problems at the time. In this book I have tried to apply the ancient Commandments to the modern era.

In addition as I studied and meditated on the Commandments I talked with many people about them and discovered that though these people all revered them, they couldn't remember them! So I preached through them in the church I pastor and broadcast a series of television shows dealing with them. The response of many people was deep and lasting.

I am greatly indebted to many authors whose names and works I have included in the list of books for suggested reading, and I would like to thank my friend Fritz Ridenour for his encouragement and Pamela Landfear for her skillful editorial work.

D. STUART BRISCOE

PLAYING

BY THE

RULES

And God spoke all these words:
"I am the Lord your God, who brought you
out of Egypt, out of the land of slavery."

Exodus 20:1, 2

Introduction

Playing by the Rules

Suppose a friend invites you to a game one Sunday afternoon in the fall, telling you he has great tickets. You know one of your favorite teams will play football in your area, so you kind of figure that's what he has in mind, even though he hasn't said so.

"Who's playing?" you ask.

"I don't know. They didn't tell me," your friend answers. That sounds kind of odd, but he has a great sense of humor, so you figure he wants to keep it as a surprise and just won't tell you now. "Where will they play?" you try to pump him.

"I thought we'd drive out to the big stadium," he tells you, and you decide you've found him out.

On Sunday you both arrive at the stadium, all psyched for a good game. Still your friend seems nervous about being in the right place and hasn't said much. So you ask the man next to you in line, "Who's playing?"

"They didn't say," he tells you.

That's funny! Could he be in my situation, too? you wonder.

11

Together you find your seats and ask around, but no one seems to know the answer. You begin to feel awfully confused.

A while later some activity starts down on the field, but you've never seen anything like it. People come out wearing all kinds of clothes, but no uniforms. Soon that doesn't seem to matter, though, because no one has a ball and no one pays any attention to the goalposts. Each person does just as he pleases. Some sit in the middle of the field, while others lie down on it. A few men run up and down, tripping on the prone and seated "players." But no one seems to know where to go or what to do. Several fellows seem to try to play one side and then the other.

Meanwhile, in the stands, some people boo softly, while others whisper a cheer. A man stands up and begins screaming for help, but everyone around him ignores him. Several more people get into a fight, and no one pays any attention. Spectators sit or stand wherever they please, paying no attention to those trying to watch the field. Not long after, in frustration, you decide to go home.

Maybe that sounds pretty bizarre, or even silly, but I'd like to submit to you that this crazy game reflects the state of our society. Today playing by the rules isn't one of the most popular ideas around. Look at the way we live—both individually and corporately.

First, you'll notice a prevailing sense of aimlessness in our communities. We lack a consensus of what we're about, of where we're going. Many varied opinions and philosophies tear us apart, until people often say, "Rules? Whose rules?" In addition our society shows an intense distaste for anything authoritative—anything that tells us what we can do, or worse, what we *can't* do.

With our inordinate desire to be free to do exactly what we please, it's hardly surprising that we should experience confu-

sion and disorientation in our society and our personal lives. Those who advocate no rules, no objectives for society, and would encourage us to do anything we want, anytime, anywhere, under any circumstances, condemn us to the same existence one of the players in the game I described might feel. Imagine yourself locked into this aimless, pointless game every day of your life. You probably *don't* have to imagine too hard, because many people recommend that kind of society today. We've seen the results.

The confusion, lack of aim, pointlessness and hopelessness in our society directly relate, I believe, to the lack of consensus that there are principles, there are rules, and that there are things we should do and ways to do them. I believe that God, in the Ten Commandments, has succinctly spelled out some things for us, and that these Commandments provide us with an excellent rule of thumb.

Where Did the Commandments Come From?

God didn't suddenly lean out of heaven and zap Moses with the Ten Commandments. No, first He moved into the life of a man called Abraham. He spoke to Abraham and promised—made a covenant with him—that He would be the God of Abraham's descendants, the seed of Abraham, and they would be God's people.

Abraham thought that a rather strange covenant, because at the time he was ninety-nine years old, and his wife, Sarah, was ninety; and they had no children. When he told his wife about it, she went off into mild hysterics at the idea. But God still stood by His promise, and as time went on Abraham and Sarah had a son. Then their son had a son, and eventually he had sons and sons and sons—and you end up with the children of Israel.

The children of Israel went into Egypt and were taken captive by the Egyptians, and they had a terrible time down there. They wailed and bemoaned their fate, and they didn't really see how they were God's people at all—God promised them a land, and they didn't have it. Where was the status He promised them? They didn't have it! He promised them all kinds of goodies—and they didn't have any of them! Instead they're stuck in Egypt.

God heard their cry and raised up Moses. He told Moses He would be their deliverer. In a mass exodus God would bring the people out of Egypt, take them through the wilderness, and place them in the Promised Land. The exodus took place, dramatically demonstrating God's grace and power.

Three months later, the people sit in the wilderness—not the most salubrious place. God calls Moses to one side and tells him to meet Him on the mountain, while the people wait at the foot of the mountain. In His meeting with Moses, He renews the covenant (Exodus 19:4-6), reaffirms their special status, and reminds them of the special land. Again He's telling them they are really His people, and He's really their God.

Now God tells Moses, "On the basis of this renewed covenant, I want you to hear some instructions—to hear some words, to hear some principles—that you must take to the people." So God gave the Ten Commandments to Moses.

What Does the Covenant Mean?

What was the point of these instructions? In Deuteronomy 6:5 (KJV), forty years after the exodus, Moses reminds the people of all these things. He makes a great statement: "And thou shalt love the Lord thy God with all thine heart, and with all thy soul, and with all thy might." This is a dominant theme of God's covenant with His people: He is their God, and they are His people. They share a love relationship.

I suspect that at some time a lot of earnest people have asked, "Excuse me, God, how do I love You?" The answer? You love God not by having a fuzzy feeling, not by having a warm glow, not by having romantic thoughts. You love God by showing that He is supreme in your life, and you show that by doing what He says. So God gives the Ten Words, the Ten Instructions, and says, "If you want to know how to love Me, do this. . . . Then you will be able to demonstrate whether or not you love Me." Having made the covenant, He speaks to Moses and says, "The people want to know how to love Me. Tell them how to do it. Give them the Ten Words."

If you check in Deuteronomy 10 and Leviticus 19, you find a second theme running through the covenant. Not only should God's people love Him, they should love their neighbors as themselves. Now we have another question: "Excuse me, who is my neighbor?" In addition, we have, "Excuse me, what does it mean to love my neighbor? Excuse me, how do I love myself, because if I don't know how I love myself, how can I love my neighbor as myself, particularly if I don't know who my neighbor is and if I don't know what loving my neighbor means?"

So God says, "Okay, Moses, give them the Ten Words. Give them the Ten Instructions. These will fill in the details, they'll put handles on the idea." God speaks to the people: It's a covenant; it's a covenant of love and grace; but He amplifies the loving relationship with the Ten Commandments.

Read Deuteronomy 6:2, 18 and you'll discover that God also feels concerned about the community living well. You might call it "the good life." People want to develop the right kind of society. How do they do it? God says, "We'll give them the Ten Words, Moses. When they do these things, they will begin to discover, to their amazement and delight, that they will have rich, full lives; their families will come together, and they will have an enriched society."

"How do we love You?" The Ten Words will help.

"How do I love my neighbor?" The Ten Words will help.

"How do we live the good life?" The Ten Words will help.

In addition the people have to have a sense of what it means to be God's people as opposed to all the other nations about them. All the other nations have laws, codes, and principles of operation. "How do we live differently from other people?" they ask. God says, "The Ten Words will help you."

Terms of the Covenant

According to some recent research on ancient treaties in the ancient Middle East, each little town had its own king. Sometimes the great king for the whole area would come along and clobber the smaller kingdoms, and the little kingdoms would end up a part of the larger territory of the more powerful king. When this happened, the great king would make a treaty with the smaller kings, which identified him as the suzerain and the smaller kings as the vassals. The treaty contained specific elements. First it told who the great king was and all about his power. The second part told how graciously and benevolently he had treated the little kings. The third part meticulously outlined how they were to live on the basis of this treaty. The fourth part ratified how it should be done, said where the copy of the treaty would be kept, and enunciated a proclamation about the treaty. The fifth part listed the blessings that would accrue to those who kept the treaty and the cursings for those who broke it. The sixth and final part invoked the gods of the nations involved to witness the signing of the treaty.

What relationship does this have to the Ten Commandments? The scholars who did this research discovered that when you compare Exodus and Deuteronomy to ancient treaties, you see that the Commandments follow the same form. As with the treaties, you can't just take the Ten Commandments out of context and expect the parts to make sense. It would be like taking the first part, defining the suzerain and vassal, out of the treaty. In the case of the Commandments, God is the great king. The people of Israel are a kingdom of priests unto God—a nation. He states His benevolence toward them, stipulates the ten principles by which He expects them to live, and gives instructions about how He expects them to live on the basis of their covenant—their treaty with Him.

What About Us?

What do the Ten Commandments mean to us today? J. I. Packer describes today's moral and ethical thinking this way: "We have assumed that self-exploration and self-discovery is a prime task, and any means to that end which does not violate others' freedom or destroy their well-being should be thought allowable, and the toleration of deviant behavior should be practiced up to the limit as being both a civilized virtue and a universal duty." But how does that theory really work in society?

Suppose you decided to go to a concert. You go to your local performing arts center and discover it's not the normal concert. For instance you notice the timpani player seems to be having a clambake in his drum—clouds of steam curl up above it. That seems rather surprising, but even worse, the tuba player has cabbages and cauliflowers growing quite nicely in his instrument. Intriguingly the harpist seems to have laundry draped over her harp.

The conductor comes on, notices all this, and insists that the three musicians clean up their act. "It won't do!" he tells them. "I will not tolerate this." So they get rid of the clambake, vegetables, and wash.

Everything's fine, right?

No, because they start to play, but as soon as the timpani

player picks up his mallet, the trumpeter gets close to him, and the drum player hits the fellow over the right ear with a resounding crack! It gives the wrong kind of sound. As the violinist brings her bow across her instrument, she sticks it right up the nose of the clarinetist.

The conductor says, "Okay, guys, come on now. Cut it out and get your act together." So everything should be okay. Right?

Not yet. The conductor raises his baton, and the brass plays the *Dead March*, the woodwinds play a gavotte, the strings play Viennese waltzes—all very beautiful, but totally chaotic.

The conductor says, "Come on, stop that! Let's play Beethoven's *Ninth Symphony*." Now they have a sense of direction. Why? He's sorted out the individual instruments; he's considered the relationship of one instrument to another; and he's developed a common theme.

At present our society says, "You don't need a common theme. We have to accept any kind of deviant behavior. We must be mature about this. If you want to do this, fine; if you want to do that, fine." But it's like letting the brass play the *Dead March* while the other instruments play their favorite pieces. We can't just go all ways. Like the orchestra, we need a consensus. We need the theme the Ten Commandments provide. We flee from them at our peril.

The Commandments and the Believer

Now this leads us to two questions. First: "Do the Ten Commandments have any significance for believers?" Some would say emphatically, "No! We're not under law, we're under grace." Others would respond, "Paul says, 'By observing the law no one will be justified.' It's right here in Galatians 2:16. We don't even have to *mention* the Ten Commandments." They both say, "The Commandments have nothing to do with us today."

Now when Paul talks about the law in that passage in Galatians, he's addressing a particular problem of the church. He had gone into all kinds of areas of the world and had told the people, "You can't get right with God by living a good life, because you can't live it good enough. If you admit you can't live it good enough, you will be open to God's forgiveness, not on your merits, but on the merits of Christ. You can be made right with God—justified—on the basis of God's free choice, not your merits; it comes by grace, by your receiving it freely through faith, not by your working at it." Paul gave this message. Lots of people believed.

Then the Judaizers came in and said, "Not so, Paul. *Real* believers adhere to all the meticulous details of the law." These guys didn't just mean the Ten Commandments. They meant over six hundred minute, nit-picking laws men had imposed on people. Really they meant, "You get right with God when you dot all your i's and cross your t's and do absolutely everything absolutely right absolutely *all* the time."

Paul says, "No, we're not under that system at all. Even if we were, works of the law couldn't justify us. We're justified by grace through faith." But he's not saying, "Listen, believers, you're under grace; that means there aren't any rules; that means anything goes."

How do we know this? Because the Lord Jesus said, "I have not come to break the law, to destroy the law, I have come to fulfill it." The word *fulfill* means literally "to give full meaning." The Lord Jesus adhered to the Ten Commandments and was the living exposition of them. Moreover Paul said that if we walk in the Spirit, we will fulfill the righteousness of the law.

Do the Ten Commandments have any significance for us today? Of course they do. Not as a means of justification, but as a means of demonstrating that we have been justified. You're not under law, you're under grace, in order that in the power of the Spirit you might fulfill the righteousness of the law as outlined in the Ten Commandments.

The Commandments and the Unbeliever

Next comes the question, "Do these laws have any relevance to unbelievers, too?" Our society comes up with all kinds of answers for this. Some say of the Commandments, "They're too simplistic. I won't accept it." Others say, "It's all relative. You need situational ethics here. One standard won't always work." A third group tells you, "The Commandments are too negative. I don't like them. Thou shalt not.... Thou shalt not...." The free spirits say, "I have to be free to be me. There's no place for these outmoded, outrageous rules." Some folks have kind of given up as far as the Ten Commandments and unbelievers are concerned.

But look at your Bible, and you'll discover that long before God made the covenant with Abraham, He used the same principles in creation. Fundamentally, God built into man's conscience the things He more sharply focuses in the Commandments. C. S. Lewis, in *The Abolition of Man*, says that if you check a number of ancient societies and cultures, you'll find surprising agreement in their ethical and moral standards, despite the widely divergent cultures. In effect he says: Man has a basic understanding of these standards that God, in creation, intends for all people.

Look at what the prophets had to say about the Ten Commandments. All along they told the people: "Get your act together and do what the Commandments say." But they predicted that not only would the covenant people of Israel adhere to these Commandments, one day God would write His laws in their hearts. That meant they would desire to fulfill His Commandments. But the prophets also said these people would come from all nations—not just the remote little group of the people of Israel, but all the nations of the world! His Commandments are meant for principles to guide individual, corporate, and general societal well-being for *everyone*. If that is true, failure to adhere to these laws, neglect of the Commandments, has results of the utmost seriousness for both believer and unbeliever.

What Do We Do With the Commandments?

Frequently Christians talk as if they really know the Commandments, but how many could write them down without pulling out their Bibles first? How many people outside the church who say they live by these laws could list them? People the length and breadth of our society *don't* know them, yet we treat them with antagonism or benign neglect at our peril.

"What do we do with the Ten Commandments?" you may ask. First, we need to use them as a compass, to give us our bearings. Many directionless people would have their lives dramatically transformed if they took the Commandments seriously.

Recently I talked to a young man. This deeply troubled fellow came to me in very difficult economic circumstances, with his life in a pretty severe mess socially. "I've had the strangest thoughts going through my mind," he told me. "I'm getting desperate financially. I wouldn't want to tell you the things I've thought."

"Like issuing worthless checks?" I asked.

"Yes, how did you know?"

"I used to be a bank examiner," I said gently. "Have you thought of holding up a bank?" He told me he had. "Is that why you're here?" He told me it was.

"I'm frightened of the voices in my head—I'm frightened of the desperation in my heart. But," he shared, "one thing holds me fast: I know it is fundamentally wrong, because the Bible says, 'Thou shalt not steal.' "

In this young man's life the Commandments acted as a bridle

to restrain him. It can work that way for others too. Even those who do not always agree with them intellectually can find these basic rules guiding their actions.

The Commandments may also act as a thermometer of our love for God. How much do we love God?—Do we have no other gods before us? Do we have no idols that we worship in His place? Do we tolerate abuse of God's name? . . . These laws evaluate our behavior to show how we love Him.

The Commandments also act as a mirror, showing us reality. As we look into the mirror of the Word of God what do we discover? The truth the Bible describes in the words "by the law is the knowledge of sin" jumps right out at us. Gazing into that mirror, we see our flaws—and those of the world around us. When society tells us we may do as we please as long as we don't step on someone else's toes, it often tells us to do what God describes in His economy as being categorically wrong. No matter how hard society tries to deny it, society is wrong, not God! When we look in the mirror, we see the reality of our own sin.

Finally the Ten Commandments can act as a guardian to bring us to Christ. Paul uses that expression. It means that the Commandments can take us only so far. They bring us to the point of realizing our own weakness and failure and sinfulness. Then they can introduce us to Christ, who alone can bring us forgiveness and the power to live differently. Someone has said the Commandments are the mirror, but not the soap. It shows me the reality of myself, but only the cleansing blood of Christ, His death on my behalf, can cleanse what the mirror shows is wrong.

We and our society need to ask the question, "Who needs the Ten Commandments?" And we both need the answer, which is simply, "You do." Then we need to be able to explain why.

You shall have no other gods before me.
Exodus 20:3

1

Who Is Number One?

When the children of Israel had only been in the wilderness about three months, God called Moses to one side and reminded him that He had made a covenant with the people of Israel and given them instructions about how they were to live. He had said He expected two basic things of them: First, they were to love the Lord their God with all their heart and all their minds and all their strength; second, they were to love their neighbors as themselves.

Like the people of Israel of old, we need a little more detail about how we can do this, and He has answered us with His Ten Words. What does it mean to love God with all our hearts? In the First Commandment we learn it means we must have Him as the Supreme One in our lives. How can we live rightly in a covenant relationship with Him? We need to have everything in subjection to Him. Loving Him with all our hearts and all our souls and all our strength means making a conscious decision to acknowledge Him as the governing factor in our lives. Loving God means that having made Him Number One in our lives, we constantly reaffirm that decision, checking to see if He still is the dominant factor there. To do that we have to be aware of the competition for His place, understand the nature of God, and make a choice.

What's the Competition?

"When you get into Canaan," God told the people of Israel, "you'll find competition—you'll find other gods that try to take My place. When you confront them, they must not be before Me [or some translations say *beside Me*]."

God wanted to prepare them for the different culture and religious structures they'd find in Canaan, and He warned them to live among the Canaanites as the unique people of God. No other gods or cultural structures should take His place. "They are not to become more important than Me; you are not to obey them rather than Me," read His message.

What about those other gods? How did they come into being? To understand that, first we have to recognize man's inborn religious instinct. Others have. Edmund Burke said, "Man is by his constitution a religious animal." Calvin approvingly quoted Cicero when he said, "There is a seed of religion planted in all men." Wherever you come across man, he never seems to feel he is the beginning and the end. No matter how well we hide this instinct, if we're honest, we'll admit we need something bigger, something other, something grander. We want something that will be beneficial to us, something that will intervene on our behalf, something to take care of us, something to look up to.

In Romans 1:18–20, the Apostle Paul makes clear God's work in all this:

> The wrath of God is being revealed from heaven against all the godlessness and wickedness of men who suppress the truth by their wickedness, since what may be known about God is plain to them, be-

cause God has made it plain to them. For since the creation of the world God's invisible qualities—his eternal power and divine nature—have been clearly seen, being understood from what has been made, so that men are without excuse.

Paul says every person on the face of the earth has at least some knowledge of there being a great power, because God makes invisible things of His Spirit plain in the order of creation. Psalm 19 says something similar. David says, "The heavens declare the glory of God," and I imagine when he wrote that he thought of those long, quiet nights he spent looking after his sheep and staring up into the sky, overwhelmed by its awesomeness and confronted by the majesty of creation. In creation he saw a picture—a demonstration—of the glory of God.

None of this implies that everybody naturally has the same understanding of the reality of God or knowledge of Him, but it does confirm that man has a religious bent. How then have we arrived at so many different conclusions, when we started off with the same instincts?

Paul tells us man has suppressed the knowledge God gave in creation. Man intends to go away from what God has shown him and resents the little he knows of God by instinct. The apostle describes these attitudes as the essence of man's wickedness.

We were created in the image of God, yet we have fallen. Because we have departed from a relationship with Him, all kinds of perversions have come into our lives, and man's undeniable ingenuity has become perverted ingenuity. Along with everything else, our religious instinct became perverted, and that has caused the many answers man provides—most of which are wrong.

When the Israelites went into Canaan, they had to confront this perversion in the form of paganism. Along with primitive peoples everywhere, the Canaanites greatly depended on natural forces. In such societies everyone keenly understands that you have to sow the seed at the right time, that the temperature has to be right, that rain needs to come at the proper time, and that soil must be fertile in order to result in a good harvest. Such people recognize what we, in our modern technological society, forget: We cannot survive in our world without these powerful natural forces.

The primitive people of Canaan tried to identify these natural forces and decided they had the power of deities. When they heard the thunder rumble, they called it the deity of thunder. When they saw the sun shine, they saw a god behind the sun. They recognized gods of fertility and fecundity. Soon they ended up with thousands upon thousands of gods, all clamoring for attention. Using their perverted religious instinct, they had put together two and two and come up with five—a pantheon of deities that formed the basis of their paganism.

The Canaanites believed that the gods of fertility, the gods of the crops, had to be appeased and placated, and they recognized a very clear link in their thinking between the fertility of the soil and the fertility of their wives. In other words crops and sex became almost synonymous. The worship of the gods of fertility became a worship of sexuality. In their perverted ingenuity, they produced all kinds of wonderfully perverted sexual activities in the name of religion. As a result, John Bright, a respected and renowned Old Testament scholar, says, "Canaanite religion presents us with no pretty picture. It was an extraordinarily debasing form of paganism."

What does this have to do with us? A lot. We live in a very sophisticated pagan culture. Just like the Israelites, we are called to be the people of God in the midst of a culture that does not honor Him. Immediately we face all kinds of problems, all kinds of attention, all kinds of opportunities. Living in our sophisticated, rational, skilled, technological society, we, too, forget the Lord. We find it so easy to develop a nominal attachment to Him, pushing Him more and more into the background as we follow the gods of society. He no longer holds the number-one spot.

What Is God Like?

In order to combat this tendency within us, God told us about Himself in His laws. He didn't give the Ten Suggestions; instead He made some powerful statements in the Ten Commandments, without introducing them in any great way. He simply comes right in and says, "Hey, folks, this is how it is. I want you to know these things."

God the Unique One

In the First Commandment, which forms the basis of the Ten Words, God reveals Himself to us. He tells us He will not accept anything less than first place in our hearts. As follow-up He gave the revelation of Deuteronomy 6:4, 5: "Hear, O Israel: The Lord our God, the Lord is one. Love the Lord your God with all your heart and with all your soul and with all your strength."

Notice "the Lord is one." How sharply that description of God's nature stands out from the religious structures of the Canaanites, who based their gods on their own rationalization! The Canaanites sat down and looked at the great forces of nature. Behind each force they identified a deity and gave it a name. Then they pulled together a pantheon of gods and tried to figure out how these gods related to one another. They quickly built a religion based on human ingenuity.

In contrast God starts with Himself, reveals Himself, and

says, "You don't have to sit down and figure out the deities, because I, the Deity, will reveal Myself to you. The Lord your God, the Lord is one."

That means two important things: First, He says He is the one and only, the absolutely unique one. To the people in the wilderness that made a lot of sense. While they lived under the Egyptians, they had a terribly hard time, but God promised to bring them out. Before He did, they had a big contest between the Lord and the gods of the Egyptians. In a nose-to-nose confrontation God had overcome the Egyptian gods. So when God said He was the one and only, they knew He claimed to be greater than all other gods.

Second, when God claimed to be one, it meant there was unity in His person. Other gods always contradicted one another. Suppose the pagans had trouble with thunder—all kinds of storms rocked the earth—and the thunder god seemed really upset. So they gave him part of their sacrifice. But the thunder god got upset at the time they needed to give the goddess of grain and fertility attention. If they sacrificed to the god of thunder, she might get upset, and then what on earth would happen when they sowed the seed? They felt torn. How could they keep all their balls in the air, trying to keep all the gods and goddesses happy?

The Lord said to the Israelites, "Hey, that doesn't happen with Me. I'm one. I don't contradict Myself; you don't get Me fighting against Myself."

God Is God

In addition to telling His people He is one, God says He is God. That means He speaks with authority. All His actions clearly demonstrate His unequivocal supremacy. To the Israelites He had already shown it in all He had done for them.

28

God Is Gracious

Finally God wants His people to remember that He is gracious. At the beginning of the Ten Commandments He reminded them, "I am the Lord your God, who brought you out of Egypt, of the land of slavery." He had shown His grace. He took a weak, helpless crowd of slaves, demoralized, disorganized, and oppressed by their captors, and intervened in their behalf. He brought them out of bondage and gave them a land they could never have claimed under other circumstances.

God reminded the Israelites of His graciousness in comparison to the other gods, whom they would have to appease. "Look what I have given you!" He declared.

One Gracious God

Living in our society, where all kinds of gods, all kinds of ideas, all kinds of philosophies abound, we desperately need such a unique, powerful, and gracious Lord. We feel tempted to follow other gods and concepts, tempted to explore them, and we may even find ourselves caught up in worshiping them. Remember we don't worship a God who brought us out of slavery, but one who intervened on our behalf through His death on a cross, saving us from death and hell. Our God has not brought us into a land of milk and honey, but gives us the gift of eternal life through His Son, our Lord Jesus. Our God has not filled the Nile with blood and frogs and all other kinds of nasty creepy-crawlies, but He has raised Jesus from the dead. Ours is the God of revelation, who commands: "Don't insult Me by bringing all the other gods alongside Me, and don't dare insult Me by putting them ahead of Me. Why? Because I am the Lord your God who brought you out of Egypt, the place of slavery, out of the bondage of sin, and I, the Lord, am one."

29

Opposition to the Commandment

God makes this powerful Commandment: "You shall have no other gods before me," yet we tend to ask, "Why not, Lord?" Well, *why* not? If we look at the Israelites' story, we can immediately see what happens if we oppose God's very nature. How quickly we fall into syncretism or sensualism!

Syncretism

Syncretism means you pull a whole lot of divergent things together to try to make a whole out of them. The children of Israel faced such a religious situation in Canaan. When they came into a town, the little king of that town would have his own special bunch of gods, the local deities. When the Israelites captured the town and overthrew the king, they met up with the temptation to gather up the gods and keep them to themselves. Then they'd have Jehovah and the gods of the town. They went into the next town—little king, little pile of gods different from all the others—they'd conquer the town and keep those gods as well. In no time at all the people of Israel can have Jehovah theoretically as their God and have a whole pantheon of gods collected on their travels. The First Commandment gets lost in the crowd.

For the same reason God warned His people not to intermarry with the Canaanites. If you married a Canaanite girl, it wasn't just marry me, marry my family. She brought along her own gods, so it meant marry me, marry my family, marry my gods. In a short time the Israelites could end up with the most unholy, syncretic mish-mash of religion imaginable. God warns them, because if they do this, forgetting the God who brought them out of Egypt, they will become utterly confused.

With our 20/20 hindsight we recognize the failings and sins of the Israelites. But what about us? We profess to honor the Lord, but our society doesn't. We listen to our society, observe it, compete in it. Whether or not we like it, we're part of it. If we want to get along in it, we think we have to listen to it, agree with it, appease it. Soon what happens? We diminish the uniqueness of the Lord. He no longer holds first place, and we end up with a syncretic Christianity.

In our syncretism, we have the audacity to want to bring in the things that are so bad that He died for them; we want the freedom to have them co-exist with the Christ who died for them. The word comes down through the centuries: "Thou shalt have no other gods before Me—thou shalt have no other gods beside Me." Why? Because Jesus is the Risen Lord. He's Number One.

Sensualism

The paganism of the Canaanites demonstrated sensuality. Man has a God-given sensuality, but like everything else in him, it's perverted. All the senses our Lord gave us He intended us to employ in understanding and appreciating Him. But we have wrongly used them in many ways. Sometimes we allow our senses to so dominate us that we push aside the truth we know, becoming purely sensual people. Now then, if the Israelites, who were a very sensual people, get into an area filled with seductively sensual paganism, those guys face some real danger. Surrounded by attractive sensuality that panders to their inner, undisciplined desires, whims, and caprices, if they don't keep on track, they will go off after other gods, will move into other areas, wandering away from the One True God. That's the problem in our society today. Our twentieth-century technological, sophisticated paganism also caters to our inner, ill-disciplined sensuality. We find it all so winsome, attractive, and utterly seductive. If we don't keep in mind that the Lord our God is one, that He has dealt graciously with us and brought us out of the house of bondage and made a covenant of grace with us, we'll end up miles from God, wrapped up in syncretism and all other kinds of things that are anathema to Him, and we'll be a religious mess! We have to honor Number One.

What's the Choice?

How do we avoid this? First we need to make a choice. In Joshua 24:14, 15 at the end of the leader's life, Joshua reminds the people of their covenant with God: "Now fear the Lord and serve him with all faithfulness. Throw away the gods your forefathers worshiped beyond the River and in Egypt, and serve the Lord. But if serving the Lord seems undesirable to you, then choose for yourselves this day whom you will serve, whether the gods your forefathers served beyond the River, or the gods of the Amorites, in whose land you are living. But as for me and my household, we will serve the Lord."

To these people who have seen the goodness, power, and grace of God, Joshua puts forth a challenge. "You are living in flat contravention of what God has said. It's time you guys shaped up! Choose this day which way you want to go."

Elijah had a similar confrontation. You'll remember he lived in the time of King Ahab, who had married Jezebel, a woman from Tyre. When she came to Ahab, the queen brought her gods with her. So we have the Tyrian gods and Jehovah—a terrible mess. Conflict arose, and in the end, Elijah stood on Mount Carmel and said to the people, "If Jehovah is God, follow Him. If He isn't, forget it. If the baals are the gods, follow them." He also comes up with this great statement: "How long are you going to waiver between two opinions?"

"You can't have your cake and your penny," he says in effect. "You can't have your cake and eat it, too."

Jesus said, "You can't worship God and mammon. You've got to decide whether or not He is Lord."

Today we face the same decision. Is God God? Is Christ Lord? If you want to acknowledge God and Christ, find out if you will follow through on the implications of that decision. Ask yourself, *What does Christ the Lord desire of me?* The answer? Unadulterated allegiance. That I should respond in love to Him because of His great love for me. *What does He deserve?* If He gave Himself for me, I should unreservedly give myself to Him. *What does Christ the Lord demand of me?* First place in my affections, that He should be the authoritative figure in my life—the one, the only, the true God. The choice is yours.

Some people have never really faced up to the absolute necessity for a basic, initial choice. "How long do you intend to waiver between two opinions?" God asks. How long do you feel you have enough of God to keep you religious, but not enough to change you? How long will you feel Christ will be satisfied with your honoring Him enough so you don't go to hell, but not honoring Him enough so you can live as if you love Him? How long will you say, "Christ is Lord," yet make it obvious about 1,001 things rate ahead of Him? "Choose," He demands.

Evaluate the Choice

Once we make that initial choice, we continually need to evaluate it. In the same way the gods of the Canaanites seduced the Israelites, the gods of our society, our cultural norms, can seduce us from the love of God.

At the end of each day, ask yourself: *Was Jesus Christ my Lord today? Did I serve Him faithfully today? Did I love Him deeply? Did I worship Him exclusively? Did I find all the other little gods in my life making unwarranted incursions into my faith? Did I live a double standard, a double life?* What will you discover? If you're honest, honoring the Lord will require a constant, disciplined walk of obedience and dependence, including repentance, restoration, and renewal.

Today I need to decide "Whom will I serve, who will be the Lord of my life?"

*You shall not make for yourself an idol in
the form of anything in heaven above or on
the earth beneath or in the waters below.
You shall not bow down to them or worship
them; for I, the Lord your God, am a jealous
God, punishing the children for the sin of
the fathers to the third and fourth generation of those who hate me, but showing
love to thousands who love me and keep
my commandments.*

Exodus 20:4-6

2

Making God
in Man's Image

Thomas Watson, the Puritan preacher, said in the seventeenth century, "In the first commandment worshiping a false
God is forbidden. In this, however, the second commandment,
worshiping the true God in a false manner is forbidden." His
few words proved a description of the essence of idolatry.

When a pastor preaches on idolatry, it can be one of the eas-
iest things he does, or it may be the hardest thing. If he takes
the easy road, he gets out a yellow legal pad, sits down, and
makes a list of all his prejudices. Then he calls them someone
else's idol. Or he might say to himself, *Now then, what do I*

really want to get after the congregation about right now? He lists the things he feels upset about with them, calls those their idols, and really lays it on them. The hard way is to try to find the underlying concern in Scripture concerning idolatry and to preach about that. I want to deal with this Commandment in the hard way, to give you a general application of Scripture that will allow the Holy Spirit to speak to your heart about these things.

God Denounces Idolatry

In the Second Commandment God clearly denounces idolatry, so we cannot mistake His reaction to it. He's not for idolatry under any guise at all and gives to His people some specific guidelines.

Don't Make Idols

Notice first of all that the Second Commandment bans the making of idols. He says to His people, "You shall not make yourself an idol in the form of anything above the earth, on the earth or beneath the waters." Some people call this "classical three-tier Hebrew cosmology," which simply means that the Hebrews thought the universe had three levels: the heavens, the earth, and the waters beneath the earth. Others apply this more specifically, saying that when you talk about creatures above the earth, it means spiritual forces; creatures on the earth means material things; what is under the earth means the denizens of death and the strange life hereafter.

No matter how you represent this description, it all comes down to one thing: In every single area of the universe, you can't use anything to represent the Creator. No material, spiritual, or strange, esoteric monster can take the place of God in your life. *Never* represent the Creator by anything created. That's the fundamental rule.

Don't Worship Idols

Second, God says, "Not only should you not make idols, you shall not bow down to them or worship them." It's one thing to make an idol and another to worship it. In the strictest sense of the term, I suppose I have some idols in my study at home.

On one occasion when I visited India, a pastor friend of mine and I got into his car. I had to move a little sack in order to sit down. When I picked it up, it clanked, and I asked, "What do you have there?"

"I'm just going to trash those things," my friend replied.

"What are they?"

He pulled one out, and I saw a beautiful piece of Indian copper work. "You're going to trash that?" I asked.

"Yes, it's a Hindu idol. The family it belonged to has just become Christians, and they have been baptized, and I'm taking their idols away. They have given them up, and I'm going to destroy them."

"I'd like to take one of them home," I told him. My friend found it hard to understand why. "It is a beautiful piece of copper work," I said, "as far as I'm concerned. It would become an idol if I bowed down and worshiped it." He gave it to me only reluctantly, with the provision that every time I saw it I would remember to pray for Hindus lost in pagan darkness.

God says, on the one hand, do not represent the Creator by anything created, but also do not render to anything that which rightly and exclusively belongs to God. Do not give to anything the worship, the adoration, the devotion that are exclusively the right and the preserve of God Himself.

That may seem strange to say to a sophisticated twentieth-century audience, but we, too, have our idols. Herbert Schlossberg said in his book *Idols for Destruction:* "Anyone with a hierarchy of values has placed something at its apex, and

37

whatever that is is the God he serves." Do you have a hierarchy of values? Of course you do. Do you say some things are good and some are bad? Some things are better and some are worse? If you answered yes, you have a hierarchy of values.

How do you distinguish good from bad? How do you measure better and worse? Somewhere along the line you have a standard of evaluation—you have the apex of your hierarchy, the thing that's most important. That, says Schlossberg, is the God you serve.

We constantly need to evaluate what forms the apex of our hierarchy. If we have rendered to it that which is exclusively God's, we have taken to idolatry.

Don't Miscalculate God's Reaction

In His denunciation of idolatry, God says, "Don't miscalculate My reaction to it." Exodus 20:5 says, "I, the Lord your God, am a jealous God." We don't like to think of that aspect of God, and many people read this far and no farther. But we need to remember that when we take all the attributes of God together, none of them are mutually incompatible. The holiness of God and the jealousy of God work together, so He exhibits a holy jealousy and a jealous holiness.

Perhaps we can understand better if we identify *jealousy* as "a zealousness for what is right, an utter, total, burning, consuming commitment to hold on to that which is right." In this sense God is jealous. With all the intensity and integrity of His being, He will defend and insist on His rightful place at the center of the universe, on the throne of His creatures' hearts. He will resist with His almighty power anything that infringes on His position.

Even more than we dislike the idea of God's jealousy, we avoid the idea that He punishes the children for the sins of the father, down to the third and fourth generations. Many people read that and respond, "If that's your God, you're welcome to Him. I'll have a different one, thank you." But think for a moment. If you go to a psychologist, chances are you'll engage in psychotherapy that will identify your emotional aberration by looking into your past. He may look at your parents and grandparents. Why? Although he may not know it, that psychologist affirms the truth of the nature of God, because to a great extent you've become what you are because of your parents' and grandparents' influence.

In effect God says, "If I do not have My rightful place in people's lives, if other things take My place, the ramifications and repercussions pass inevitably from generation to generation." Again He denounces idolatry.

Don't Forget God's Grace

In addition God says, "Don't forget My grace!" In marked contrast to the statement about punishing the children, He goes on to say, "I show love." (The Hebrew word here is *hesed*, meaning "love, mercy, grace, kindness"; it's an all-encompassing, beautiful covenant word of the Old Testament.) He shows this love, kindness, mercy, and grace to thousands. The structure of the Hebrew here contrasts three or four generations with thousands of generations. Remember, when God speaks firmly, He also remains ready to act graciously, and His grace is always infinitely greater than His judgment. Paul puts it this way, "Where sin [and accordingly judgment] abounds, grace much [or *hyper*] abounds" (see Romans 5:20).

Be on Your Guard!

Not only did God address this issue in the Commandments, He also mentions it throughout Scripture. The prophets also have a number of trenchant words about idolatry. Remember, God warned the children of Israel, coming into the Promised

Land, to avoid the gods of the Canaanites. If you look at the ministry of the prophets, you'll realize the children of Israel ignored this warning. As Jeremiah 10: 2–5 says:

> Do not learn the ways of the nations or be terrified by signs in the sky, though the nations are terrified by them. For the customs of the peoples are worthless; they cut a tree out of the forest, and a craftsman shapes it with his chisel. They adorn it with silver and gold; they fasten it with hammer and nails so it will not totter. Like a scarecrow in a melon patch, their idols cannot speak; they must be carried because they cannot walk. Do not fear them; they can do no harm nor can they do any good.

The books of other prophets hold many similar passages, reminding God's people of the powerlessness of the idols God denounces. Yet the Israelites had an amazing propensity to simply move their lives into the worshiping of powerlessness and into the abandonment of themselves to the worthless and meaningless. Their prophets warned them to avoid it like the plague.

In the New Testament Jesus doesn't say much about idolatry, except for His statement, "You cannot serve God and mammon. You cannot worship two masters—you'll love one and hate the other" (see Matthew 6:24). He said little about idolatry because the people He ministered to didn't have a problem with that.

But when Paul moved out into the Gentile world, he found all kinds of idolatry. He faced it with the Corinthians, who offered meat to idols. Today we say, "Who cares?" The Corinthian Christians cared. Paul certainly cared. The pagan people would offer their meat offering to idols—prime rib, corn-fed, the best beef—nothing but first class for the idols. But the

the idols had little appetites, and the priests had big appetites, so the priests left a little for the idols and took most for themselves. They still had far more than they could handle, so they took some down to the butchers. The butchers sold it to the restaurants, so if you wanted a good meal and took your friends from Ephesus to the best restaurant in town, when you ordered prime rib, you got meat offered to idols.

The Christians said, "We can't go to restaurants. We can't order the best cuts of meat, because this is all involved in idolatry." They saw it as a big issue.

What did Paul say? The apostle told them, "The idols are nothing in themselves, but demonic powers lie behind them. Be on your guard about idolatry because of those powers behind the idols, which will sidetrack you from God. Stay on your toes, because you could innocently get yourself into trouble this way." But in Colossians and Ephesians, he says that "greed or covetousness is idolatry." Why? Because greed and covetousness mean I've given myself in utter devotion to the created thing rather than to the Creator.

The Dangers of Idolatry

"Hey, what's the big deal about all this?" you may ask. Maybe you still feel like the little boy who had supper with his parents one night and let slip a little word he'd learned in school that day. He wanted to practice it. Dad, who heard that word often in the office, didn't even notice, but his mother acted horror struck, banished him from the table, and told him to stay in his room all night.

After the boy had gone to his room, a terrible thunderstorm blew up. The lightning flashed and thunder crashed; the rain came slashing down, and the mother's heart went pitter-pat, as she wondered how her child was. She crept up to his bedroom and quietly opened the door. There she saw her small boy, silhouetted against the window, and heard him say, "God, all this for one little word?"

Do you feel as if God's become somewhat overreactionary to idolatry? *Is* it a big deal? Emphatically, yes! "Why?" you ask. Because idolatry *is* dangerous and may affect your spiritual life in seven ways.

Turning Means Into Ends

If all people have some instinctive knowledge of God's existence, they want to respond to Him. But when they look for ways to do that and turn to their culture and the things they make and begin to use their ingenuity to produce things to help them understand the invisible, they enter into idolatry. As they use tangible things to reach out to the intangible, the things take the place of the intangible, and the means become an end in themselves. They do exactly what God says not to do: The created takes the place of the Creator.

That may sound strictly pagan, but it doesn't make Christians exempt. Have you ever noticed that, though we use many methods to worship God, sometimes they become so important to us that we lose all sight of the God we worship, and the forms become an end in themselves? For example, at one time most people couldn't read, so the church developed a liturgy to help everyone memorize Scriptures. That was very helpful. But when, as often happens, the liturgy became worshiped instead of God, it lost its helpfulness.

I don't mean that as a shot at liturgy—every church has some form of liturgy—but it shows how, in the life of the Christian, the created may begin to take the place of the Creator.

Substituting Things for People

Next, idolatry makes things more important than the person. God has not revealed Himself as a power or entity or a thing, but as a person with whom we can relate. We share a friendship in which we know Him, love Him, and respond in gratitude to Him. But the idolator makes a mistake in substituting things for Him. Initially he may even put good things in God's place, but by his doing that, those things become bad. Even a ministry may begin to replace the Lord in importance—I know, because I've done it!

At one stage in my career, it looked as if my preaching days had ended. Although I had been at it for many years, tremendous new opportunities had begun to open before me. I stood right on the edge, when I suffered an illness that threatened to stop it all. For the only time I can remember I suffered depression. I did not feel at all happy with the situation. My concern, I told myself, stemmed from the fact that I loved to preach about the Lord Jesus. Then in my own heart God spoke to me powerfully, saying, "Stuart Briscoe, do you love preaching about the Lord Jesus more than you love the Lord Jesus about whom you preach?" The answer was yes. I knew I felt upset with the Lord Jesus because I could not preach about Him. If I had been excited about Him, it would not have mattered whether or not I could have preached about Him. I felt as if the Spirit of God said, "You get things in perspective, and we might let you preach again. *Until* you get it in perspective, you'll never preach."

When a good thing becomes overimportant to us, it becomes our possession. We get so excited about it that we worship ourselves rather than the Lord, as in the case of my ministry, which had turned into idolatry; that sin destroyed its effectiveness.

Placing Imagination Above Revelation

In addition idolatry places man's imagination above God's revelation. Look at some of the representations of the gods made by various cultures, and their creators' imagination will amaze you. Some Egyptian gods have the figure of a human being but the head of a crocodile, or ox, or lion. When those men thought of a sudden and fierce god, nothing seemed more sudden and fierce in anger than a crocodile. Nothing seemed more brave and courageous than a lion—and so on. So they used their imagination to create fantastic gods that represented these concepts.

Surely God has given us imagination, but our imagination, too, is fallen. It's not pure and clean, but easily becomes warped and twisted. How? By our thinking, which does not follow God's truth, but our own fantasies. As J. I. Packer has said, "Metal images are the consequence of mental images." Instead of accepting himself as a man made in God's image, the idolator tries to remake God in his own image. He tries to bring Him down to a "comfortable" size.

What happens if we do this? Our imagination begins to destroy our lives as we turn from His truth to our fantasy, for we find ourselves estranged from the real world, divorced from truth.

As Christians we may do this by trying to turn God into some kind of celestial Santa Claus. We don't like the God of Scripture and much prefer the one in our fantasy world. In making ourselves comfortable, we totally destroy reality as far as God is concerned. We have put in God's place that which we manufactured ourselves.

Limiting God's Transcendence

Idolatry also imposes limits on divine transcendence. When Solomon created the temple, he felt awestruck by the magnificent building until God deigned to enter it. Then he lost interest in physical surroundings. He worshiped the Lord, declaring, "God, even the heaven of heavens cannot contain you. Will you deign to live in a place made by human hands?" (see 1 Kings 8:27). He had the right idea.

The idolator thinks, *This thing I have created contains God. This thing I devote myself to, this thing for which I live, this thing for which I will give myself—this is God.* What happens? The great, transcendent God becomes squished down into a totally insulting situation.

We Christians cut God down to our own size, destroying reverence. For example, in church have you ever seen a parent collect the kids from the nursery and take them to the sanctuary? The kids start running around, jumping and dancing, parading up and down the steps. Mother comes rushing up, saying, "Don't do that! This is God's house."

The kids start looking around. "Where is God? Is He in the booth back there? Is He in that box?"

Are they really in God's house? No. But some people would like the church to be God's house, because then they could keep Him in there, visit Him once a week, like a sick relative, and run their lives the way they want to. They've brought God down to their own size.

Putting Man in Control

Idolatry places man in control of God, but at a terrible price. Isaiah describes what had happened to his people this way, "Your idols have become a burden to you." His words would have reminded the Hebrews of the actions of the Babylonians—a pagan people who had conquered them and taken them into captivity. Wherever they went, the Babylonians carried their idols with them. Isaiah 46 compares the idolatry of the Hebrews to that when it says, "Listen, your idols are a burden to you, because you carry them," but it goes on to remind them, "But when God brought your forefathers out of Egypt, He carried them."

Who carries whom means a lot. If I worship idols, I carry them. I control my God. Because I've made Him small, I can put Him where I want. He won't intrude on my life.

But look at the repercussions of that in my life. If man controls God, it means he is god. If I'm god, then God help us. Like the self-made man, who deifies himself, I will worship my creator—myself. Like the self-made man, I will get terribly upset when others don't come and worship at my church, the "First Church of Stuart Briscoe." Every day I will invite others to idolatry and become terribly upset when they don't share my vision of myself. If, as such a church implies, man is the beginning and the end, we are of all creatures most miserable.

Fashioning God in a Popular Style

Idolatry fashions God in the popular style, making Him suit the world around us. See how it happened with the children of Israel. While all the nations around them developed polytheism, they stood out because they believed in one God, who had revealed Himself to them.

When He made the covenant with them, God warned His people against syncretism, but they didn't listen. In the end they became so confused, they called Jehovah "Baal." By then they had lost sight of their unique convenant relationship with Him. Finally they so degenerated that they even threw their children into the fiery furnaces of the pagan god Moloch. The Israelites had remade God in the contemporary style.

When we do this in our lives, we totally destroy our distinctiveness as the people of God. How can we be distinguished from the antichrist, antigod society surrounding us? The Christian church always faces the tension of holding to the eternal revelation yet communicating it to today's world. Some of us easily remain relevant but lose faithfulness. Others may stay faithful and lose relevance. We all need to ask: *How can I be faithful to the Word of God and relevant to a society that does not know Him—or even want to know Him?*

Each of us faces this tension not to get so caught up in our culture that we lose sight of the Lord. If we do so, we finish up as strangers to Scripture, unknown in the courts of heaven.

Detracting From God's Image

Finally idolatry detracts from God's chosen image. If we remake God in our image, we have forgotten that God made man in His image, that the image was marred, and that He sent Christ, the express image of His person. If I make up my own images, I ignore Christ. I will not understand the unique place God gave man, and my idolatry will denigrate my understanding of man and will depreciate my experience and appreciation of Christ.

All our idolatry attempts to whittle God down, suit Him to our way of doing things, fit Him in a "comfortable" pattern that does not harm our own ideas or challenge our way of thinking. By the time we have finished, we have denied God His power, muddied or defaced His image, and left ourselves with pitiful, empty lives that benefit neither Him nor us.

Idolatry's serious business. God cannot ignore it. Man does so at his peril!

*You shall not misuse the name of the Lord
your God, for the Lord will not hold anyone
guiltless who misuses his name.*

Exodus 20:7

3

Using God
for My Own Ends

Most of us are familiar with the text of the Third Commandment in the King James Version translation: "Thou shalt not
take the name of the Lord thy God in vain...." Chances are
that we have used the expression "taking the name of the Lord
in vain." But what do we mean when we say it?

If we talk to most regular churchgoers about the meaning of
that Commandment, they'll probably tell us it has something to
do with bad language, with cursing and swearing and profan-
ity. When you start to talk about it, most of them will relax,
knowing they don't do anything like that—at least not often.

In saying that, though, they have missed something important. There's much more in the idea of this Commandment
than we've commonly allowed for.

What's in a Name?

What's in a name? I want to try to answer that question with
particular reference to "the name of the Lord"—the thing we

have been warned not to take in vain. What does a name mean, and how do we misuse it?

Reputation

Generally we can say that a name speaks of the reputation of the person who bears it. In the Bible we see examples of lots of different reputations based on names. In Genesis 11, the story of the tower of Babel, we learn that the people had come together in a large city with the objective of making a name for themselves. They planned to build a tower that would reach up into the heavens; they wanted to look good for their own gain. In effect they said, "We don't really need God; we can handle this thing ourselves, and we will establish our own reputation, irrespective of God."

"Is it always wrong to make a name for yourself? Didn't the writer of the Proverbs say a good name is more to be desired than riches? Where does Scripture say you can't make a name for yourself?" you may ask. In that verse the writer of Proverbs meant that a good reputation, in the long run, has a lot more value than money. Many people have made lots of money and ruined their reputations doing it. Others have impeccable reputations, but have never translated that into funds. The verse says: "If you've got to choose, always choose the good name, the good reputation." He didn't encourage anyone to look good for his own gain, but not to put money before honor.

Philippians 2 tells us that God gave the Lord Jesus a name which is above every name, that at the name of Jesus every knee shall bow and every tongue confess that He is Lord. That speaks of His powerful reputation.

The people in Scriptures understood this concept of reputation. When they named their children, they did it very carefully. Sometimes they named a child for something that reflected the desires they had for him. Other times they gave him a name that related to a circumstance of his birth. In all cases they looked well at the meaning of the name a child would bear before they gave it to him.

My own name has something of a special significance in this way. Just before I was born, my father picked up a book called *In the Heart of Savagedom*, the story of two single women who worked as missionaries in the Belgian Congo. These intrepid ladies took off into the wild blue yonder and got into all kinds of hair-raising escapades. It was a very exciting book, and my dad got inspired by these two single women who single-handedly took on the whole Belgian Congo.

He said to my mother, who was not particularly interested in reading a book but was interested in getting rid of me, "If this kid's a boy, we'll call him Stuart," because one of the missionaries had the name Eva Stuart Watt. My father hoped something of this intrepid missionary would rub off on me. When I was small, my dad told me the story, and I've always borne it in mind.

Many years later I preached in Belfast, Northern Ireland; at the end of the service I stood at the rear of the church and shook hands with everyone as they left. At the end of the line came a tiny, wizened old lady, carrying an umbrella with which she reinforced her points—and she had a lot of points she wanted to make to me. She began to poke me with her umbrella as she said, "Our pastor's no good . . . no good. You come be our pastor."

"Well," I said, "I don't think he would like it if I just arrived and said, 'Okay, I'm going to be your pastor.' You can't do it that way."

"He's no good," she told me again. She really wasn't too high on her pastor. "They don't like me in this church, either. They just don't like me."

"Oh," I said, "I'm sure—"

"No," she told me emphatically, "they don't. Don't say they do, when I tell you they don't."

"All right, why would they not like you?"

"It's the prostitutes I bring in," she replied forthrightly.

"You bring in prostitutes?"

"Yes, they're gorgeous, gorgeous prostitutes, and I bring them to church. They're beautiful girls. They've got terrible stories, and they need the Lord Jesus; but when I bring them into church, all those people move out. They don't want to sit next to them. I love these prostitutes."

I enjoyed this intrepid little old lady, who told me, "I think you would like them, too. If you would come and be our pastor, you'd be fine with our prostitutes." She did most of the talking, and we only began to end our conversation after the church had been empty about half an hour. As I left I asked her name. "I'm Eva Stuart Watt's sister," she told me. I felt excited to meet her and told her my story. After that it took me another half hour to convince her I wouldn't come be their pastor.

What's in a name? Reputation—in my family Eva Stuart Watt had one for her missionary zeal that could not be dimmed by circumstances. Her name said something about what you could expect from her.

Character

A name could also be a prophetic statement in terms of a child's character. The Jews knew this. "Thou shalt call His name Jesus." Why? Because lots of kids had the name Jesus? No, "thou shalt call His name Jesus," not because it was a common name, derived from *Joshua*, but because it meant "savior." The character of the Son of God was built into that name.

Personality

A name may also speak of the personality involved. Sometimes personalities change, as we see in the story of Jacob.

Jacob wrestles with God—a silly thing to do. He wrestled all night, and in the end God let him do what he wanted. God gives you a lot of room to wrestle with Him, but in the end, He said, "I've just got to be getting on to someone who's going to be more responsive." So He clinked Jacob's thigh out of joint.

If you've taken part in the sport, you know that once your thigh goes out of joint, you kind of lose interest in wrestling. So Jacob lay down and said, "Okay. I've been resisting You, now I'll rely on You." God says, "All right, that's fine. Your name is *Jacob*, but it will be *Israel*." The Lord detected a change in this man. *Jacob* means "crook, slimy character." *Israel* means "prince of God." What's in a name? It describes what you're like.

Authority

A name also carries a sense of authority. In the beginning God created the world. How did He do it? First He said, "Let there be light." By the very naming of it, it came into existence. He made everything out of nothing—even the names. But the names held a significance. In the giving of the name is authority.

He made Adam and told him, "All right, Adam, now there're lots of animals around here. It's your responsibility to name them." In this way God said, "I have authority over the whole of creation. I'll delegate a lot of it to man, and man will demonstrate that authority in the naming of these things."

God's Name

How do reputation, character, and authority relate to the name of the Lord? You remember that in the Old Testament God reveals Himself by His name, in marked contrast to the false gods all around. The false gods, instead of telling men their names, received names from their creators. As a man gave a god its name, he also gave it personality, character, and a reputation. It all resulted from human ingenuity, man imposing his wishes on his gods.

God Is Knowable

But when God revealed His name, He took the initiative, saying, "Man, you can't make Me the way you want Me to be. I am. As the 'I am' I will demonstrate who I am, so that you will have no questions about it." He chooses to let us know Himself in His true nature.

When God introduces Himself to Abraham or Moses or anyone else, in effect He says, "I'm knowable. I want to introduce Myself to you."

Americans are great at introducing themselves. When I first came to America, over twenty years ago, I remember going into the Deep South. The very first time I preached, a great big man came up to me and said, "Hi, I'm Bill." At first I didn't understand what he'd said, but I got it interpreted that he was saying, "Hello, my name is Bill." Then he shook hands and became very intimate with me. Bill grabbed me and put his arm around me; then at the end of the talk he gave me a big hug. Now the British are terribly proper, and nobody had ever done that to me, probably not even my father. Being so terribly proper, that sort of thing isn't necessary. This person who came and identified himself kind of took me aback, because he opened himself up to me so quickly. From that I learned a lot about him.

As soon as I introduce myself to somebody, I reveal my identity, saying, "Hey, folks, I am knowable." God does the same thing. When He names Himself, He invites us to know Him in a special way. Remember, when He revealed Himself to the patriarchs, He really said, "This is who I am. Study My name. It will give you My reputation, My character, and a feel for My authority. These will give you an opportunity for intimacy with the living God."

Daniel says that they who know their God shall be strong and do exploits. Why? Because they have an intimacy of relationship with God.

Remember the young David, chomping at the bit because his big brothers had gone off to war and he had to stay home? One day his mom said, "Okay, you can go to war. Take this bag of cookies to your big brothers." So David went off, hating that bag of cookies, but glad he could go. When he got to the campsite of the army, he found all his brothers and all the other big soldiers cowering in the bottom of a trench. Out on the hillside stood a big giant, saying, "Come on, your champion shall fight me. If I win, my side wins. If you win, your side wins."

What an excellent way of settling international differences. Only the Philistines wanted to do it that way, because they had Goliath. The Israelites weren't in a hurry to answer that challenge. David, the teenager, asked his brothers, "Why don't you have a go at it?"

They answered, "Mind your own business."

"Why don't you go?" Nobody was interested.

David asked so insistently and persistently, that in the end word got to King Saul. King Saul stood head and shoulders over anyone else. Guess who should have gone out to Goliath? "No way!" said Saul. So in the end young David prevailed on King Saul to let him go.

I can't believe Saul let him go. But he did what adults do when teenagers embarrass them. He tried to put David in his own armor, lowered him inside, clamped it shut, and screwed down the helmet. Out of that tin can a little voice cried, "Let me out of here!"

When they let David out, he said, "I don't need all that stuff." He went to a brook and got five smooth stones, wound up his sling, and flexed his wrist, elbow, and shoulder. He sauntered up to Goliath, who just stood there with his spear like a weaver's beam. Goliath asked David, "Am I a dog? Am I a dog that you should come to me like that?"

David answered, "No, you're no dog. You're a very big giant. I've come to get you ... come to get you."

Goliath's deep voice rumbled, "You've come with your sword and spear?"

David calmly replied, "No, but I come to you in the name of the Lord." What does he mean? "You can keep your swords, your spears. I come with the intimate knowledge of the living God." David knew the power of God; he relied on His force, His initiative, His protection.

God Saves Us

When we know God and His protection, live intimately with Him, coming to terms with Him as He is, we experience His salvation. David certainly did in his battle with Goliath. The apostle Paul, writing to the Corinthians, says that through faith in His name we are saved. Does that mean you use His name like abracadabra—"Jesus, Jesus, Jesus"—magic? No. It means that in God's revelation, as we put our faith in Him as He really is, not as we wish He were, the power of His salvation becomes released in our lives. When that happens, you have the opportunity to be identified with Him through His name.

Saul of Tarsus traveled along the road to Damascus when suddenly a bright light smote him. In that light he saw the risen Christ. Suddenly he realized Christ was for real. He fell on his face, saying, "Lord, what would you have me do?" The now blind man went into Damascus, waiting because the Lord needed someone to minister to him. No one felt terribly enthusiastic about ministering to Saul of Tarsus. Why? Because to minister to him meant you could sign your own death warrant. It was suicidal.

God found a little man called Ananias. "What are you doing, Ananias?"

"Just packing, Lord,"

"Where you going?"

"I don't know, I'm just getting out of here."

"Why, Ananias?"

"Because Saul of Tarsus is coming, Lord, and he's a nasty, nasty gentleman. He doesn't like followers of the Way. He doesn't like those who bear Your name, Lord. He exterminates them one by one. I may be next."

"Well, before you run, Ananias, I have a little job for you."

"What is that, Lord?"

"I'd like you to do a little witnessing."

"It won't take long, will it?"

"No, it won't take long at all."

"To whom shall I go?"

"Saul of Tarsus."

Ananias went. He entered the room with great trepidation. To his intense delight, he saw that Saul was blind. The Lord said, "Lay your hands on him, Ananias—not around his neck, Ananias—on his head."

Ananias laid his hand on Saul's head and started with two beautiful words, "*Brother Saul,* I've come to tell you that God has chosen you to bear His name. And I'm also here to tell you how great things you must suffer for His name."

What did Ananias mean? God has revealed His name, shown that He is knowable, invites us to intimacy, promises power and protection in the knowledge of His name, and gives us the privilege of putting His name upon ourselves. As we do that we so identify with Him that we bear the privilege of making the knowable God known. We bear His name, but not without cost.

Dave Ramsdale is a missionary pilot in South America. Together we got into a little float plane on an oxbow lake, which lies off one of the headwaters of the Amazon River. As we took off I began to talk with Dave; flying over the impenetrable jungle, he told me we might visit one of the primitive Indian tribes he ministered to. He also said he had flown professionally on his last furlough and had the ratings and skills to fly out of the busy New York City area airports.

I looked below at a landscape that didn't look the least like New York City. Eventually we landed in a little jungle creek. While we visited the Indians, we covered our legs with sulphur, to keep the mosquitoes from eating us alive.

Getting back into the plane, I asked Dave why, with all his skill, he chooses to fly in the middle of nowhere. In effect he told me it's a privilege to bear the name of Jesus to people who have never heard it. Despite all the hardship, he stays on for the privilege of bearing the name.

How Do We Take His Name in Vain?

Even though we understand all this about God's name, how have we at times taken it in vain? How do we still misuse it? Remember the word *vanity* occurs quite a lot in the Old Testament. It means "to empty of content, to make irrelevant." How can I take the name of the Lord and empty it of content? When have I made it irrelevant? What have I done to take the name of the Lord and twist it into shapes He never intended it to go in? That's what this Commandment talks about.

Well, the folks in the Old Testament did a pretty good job at this kind of thing. Then they often took oaths. Today, before you can borrow money from someone, he'll check on your credit rating; he wants empirical evidence that you'll repay.

The Israelites didn't have credit ratings. How did a man know if you'd repay his loan? You'd take an oath, calling on the name of the Lord. You'd say, "The Lord do so-and-so to me, also, if ..., unless...." That's where the phrase "as the Lord liveth" became so popular; they had all kinds of expressions to show their dependence on God to control the results of the promise.

What they originally meant was I'm promising this, knowing that the Lord God knows everything, including this promise. I'm taking this oath knowing that God is my judge. God knows I'm making this promise, and He will judge me if I don't keep it. That kind of oath had profound significance.

What happened? Well, you know how people get casual. After a while they would call on the name of the Lord when they didn't mean it. They would say, "As the Lord liveth ...," but they were just empty words. Although they spoke His name, they didn't think of His oversight. When they used His name in their oaths, they no longer considered their accountability to Him. They emptied His name of consequence.

The people of God identified with Him in many ways, but they no longer lived as His people should. God says, "I won't hold anyone guiltless who empties My name of its meaning, who calls on My name but shows deep in his heart he could care less about Me." Acting as if you cared about His oversight when you really don't insults God. When you do that, you say in your heart, "Phooey to you, God," and God won't hold you blameless for it.

Making a Name for Ourselves

One of the ways we can take the Lord's name in vain is to try to make a name for ourselves. We may engage in activities "in the name of the Lord" yet have a mixed-up motivation. Instead of honestly doing it for Him, we do it for ourselves. Though we talk about His name, we do it for ours.

Maybe you've seen this in people who proclaim that they're doing this and that in the name of the Lord, but get all bent out of shape when they don't get the glory. If they don't get a pat on the back, their noses get bent out of shape. If they don't get honored or when someone else gets "their" chance, they get all upset. Why? Because they don't really care for the name of the Lord—they care for themselves.

Praying for Our Benefit

Though we may not have sworn since the last time mother cleaned our mouths out with soap, lots of us have still taken the Lord's name in vain by praying in His name for our exclusive benefit. Someone has said that one reason we don't seem to have prayers that work is that we put all our begs in one ask-it. When we get together in our churches and tag the end of our prayers with "in the name of Jesus" or "for Jesus' sake, amen," if they're all our ask-its, what have we really said? We've told God, "Hey, I want this, and I want it for me," then at the end we try to turn it around and say, "but it's really for You, Jesus." He knows it isn't at all.

God can't forget this, can't ignore it, and can't go around it. By calling His what isn't His at all and ignoring what is His we've emptied His name of significance. Instead of putting it all in His hands, we've tried to manipulate God to do it our way. We've taken His name in vain while pretending to take part in one of the most powerful resources He's given us: prayer.

Not Committing Ourselves to His Control

When we call on God without committing ourselves to His control, we misuse His name. Members of Congress are allowed the privilege of sending their official mail free, so long as the envelope clearly states that it contains material related to congressional affairs. Some unscrupulous people have seen a way to save some bucks by printing similar envelopes for their own use. They have committed a crime in so doing, because of the abuse of the name.

It is a sobering thought that even God's servants can make false claims to be operating in His name when in actuality they are repudiating His control. Clearly there is much more involved in "taking the name of the Lord in vain" than cussing and swearing!

Remember the Sabbath day by keeping it holy. Six days you shall labor and do all your work, but the seventh day is a Sabbath to the Lord your God. On it you shall not do any work, neither you, nor your son or daughter, nor your manservant or maidservant, nor your animals, nor the alien within your gates. For in six days the Lord made the heavens and the earth, the sea, and all that is in them, but he rested on the seventh day. Therefore the Lord blessed the Sabbath day and made it holy.

Exodus 20:8–11

4

This Is the Day

The Lord God spoke these words of the Fourth Commandment to Moses, who passed them on to His covenant people, the people of Israel, at Mount Sinai. As a sign of their love for Him, He commanded the Israelites to follow His law about work and leisure time. "Six days," He told them, "you shall work, and the seventh day—the leisure time—you shall keep holy."

Now we all recognize work and leisure time as integral parts of our lives, and it's encouraging to notice God has some specific words for us on this subject. However many people don't understand we can demonstrate our relationship to the Lord by the way we work and use our leisure time, that these things do reflect our feelings about Him.

Some folks regard work as drudgery. Every morning they drag themselves out of bed and go to work, hating every minute of it, so disgruntled they just can't wait to get out of their jobs and enjoy the weekend. They belong to the "Thank God it's Friday" school of theology.

Does God support that? No! Only if you base your theology on the Fall—when work became drudgery for man—will you treat work as a necessary evil. If you base your theology on creation, you have no case for that attitude at all. In creation we see that God labored; therefore labor is good and right and proper. After man's creation, God also gave him work on the face of the earth; therefore the way we work will show our attitude toward Him. We do better to avoid the ideas of the TGIF classmates and to follow Paul's command, "Whatever you do, do it heartily as unto the Lord . . ." (see Colossians 3:23).

However, the Fourth Commandment spends most of its time dealing with leisure, not work. How are we to regard the Sabbath and keep it holy?

Remember the Sabbath

First God says, "Remember the Sabbath day." What does that mean for us today? Obviously, we do not operate in the same circumstances as the Israelites to whom He first gave this Word. They had just escaped from Egypt; they were slaves on the run, a nomadic people. As they moved through the wilderness, for them a successful day meant one in which they survived. They didn't even know if they would make it into the Promised Land.

Today few of us think purely in terms of survival, because many things in our culture aid us in doing a whole lot more than staying alive. How do today's work and expanded leisure time fit with the Fourth Commandment? As technology increases, it becomes clear that whether or not we like it we're going to have more leisure time to use or abuse.

The Inauguration of the Sabbath

God did not introduce this idea at Mount Sinai. Remember, He gave the Ten Commandment principles to the children of Israel before that. While they traveled through the wilderness, His people didn't have food, so God sent manna.

Manna is an interesting word. Literally it means "What is it?" It simply arrived every morning, and people looked out of their tents and said, "What is it?" *Manna*. The name stuck. When mother prepared it and put it on the table, the kids did what kids always do. They turned up their noses and said, "What is it?" Mother said, "Just eat your 'What is it?' and enjoy it."

Now manna came every morning, but as soon as the sun came up, it melted away. Moses told the people to gather only enough for one day. If they took too much, it began to go off, and everybody knew they'd been greedy. But on the sixth day, they got twice what they needed for the day. Some of the authorities saw this, came to Moses, and complained. Moses said, "That's all right, the Lord told them to, because on the seventh day they are to do no work. It is a Sabbath unto the Lord."

On Mount Sinai, in the Fourth Commandment, God confirms the Sabbath. It's interesting to take a look at how, through the history of Israel, He amplified this idea. In Exodus 16 they are not to go outside to collect manna. In Exodus 34, when the people have become farmers and have settled down, they are told that when it's seedtime, you don't sow your seed on the Sabbath,and during harvesttime, you don't harvest the crop.

I remember having many farmer friends when I grew up. They went to little Methodist chapels, where I used to go preach often, and they would always attend, even on Sundays in harvesttime. Now in England, harvesttime is absolutely critical, because the country gets very little of the hot, dry weather which is suitable for harvesting. So when they got a hot, dry day, everybody would drop everything, rush into the fields, and grab what harvest they could. But the old Methodist farmers refused point-blank to gather their harvest on a Sunday.

Many times I've seen it rain every day of the week and clear up on Sunday. All the unbelievers would go out and harvest their crops, laughing at the believers who left their crops standing. The Christians operated on the basis of faith. That's what the Lord called the children of Israel to do: When they were in the wilderness, no going out of where they lived; when they farmed, no farming on the Sabbath day.

Now this Sabbath idea seemed great for the men, because they got one day in seven off, but they told their wives to get on with work as usual. The Lord said, "Uh-uh, that's not the way to go. We will have no domestic activity either." So in Exodus 35 we find a restriction about building fires on the Sabbath day. If you go to orthodox Jewish homes today, they will not light a fire on the Sabbath. Many of them get around that by bringing in a Gentile to do the job. But they still adhere to that rule.

What was the point? By prohibiting fires, God illustrated the concept that the domestic people should have the day off, too.

In Jeremiah 17 the people now have developed their economy. They don't all farm. So in order to give rest to those who engage in business, who do warehousing and trading, now they cannot carry burdens on the Sabbath day.

God simply applies the same rule to their differing situations. He says, "Six days you do your work; on the seventh day— under no exceptions—you don't work." He further amplifies it to say that strangers who are not Jews who live among them shall not work either, nor shall the animals. "Every seventh year the land shall be given a total rest as well," God says, too. "It shall lie fallow. And on the seventh of the seven-year cycle, the forty-ninth year, you will introduce the Year of Jubilee, when everything will be specially laid fallow."

A lot of study has gone into trying to find out how we arrived at a seven-day week, and many people have come up with various ideas from different cultures. No matter what we feel about how we got a seven-day week, no other people suggested that one day in seven should remain totally free from activity. We can only attribute that to the Jewish people, and they attribute it to God and His concern for mankind.

Why a Sabbath?

The Fourth Commandment describes the Sabbath as being based in creation: God created everything in six days, and on the seventh He rested. He was refreshed and reflected on all He had done. He rejoiced in all He had achieved.

But Scripture also gives three additional reasons for the Sabbath freeing people from all work activities.

For Humanitarian Reasons

If you take the idea of the Sabbath as it is in Leviticus 25, God seems to say that the one day of rest in seven has its humanitarian reasons. You cannot keep a violin strung at concert pitch all the time; if you do, it will break. You cannot keep people going seven days a week; you cannot keep animals going seven days a week; you cannot farm your land year after year. If you do these things, it all falls apart. Therefore God ordained a day of rest.

To Show Trust in God

In Deuteronomy 5, where Moses reiterates the Ten Commandments as the people prepare to go into the Promised Land, he says they are to remember the seventh day because God brought them out of Egypt.

If these people stop working one day in seven, everybody around will say, "Are these people crazy? Are they nuts? They'll never make it. They can't possibly survive." Today many business people talk like that. If you have a whole row of shops that stay open seven days a week, and one of the shop-owners decides not to open, the others will say, "He's crazy. It's only a matter of time until they will close him down, and he'll go into bankruptcy." Just as they no doubt said of the children of Israel!

Why did God tell them to take off one day of the week? Because through that they demonstrated their trust in and dependence upon the Lord. Why should they do that? Because He had brought them out of Egypt. The one day in seven showed how grateful they felt toward Him that on their behalf He had come through over and over again.

As a Sign of the Covenant

Finally Exodus 31 tells us the Sabbath is a sign of the covenant. Remember that when God made the covenant, He ordained the circumcision as its sign. This outward and visible change reflected an inward and spiritual experience. Most people know that, but do not know that the Sabbath also was a sign of the covenant.

God said, "I love you. I will be your God; demonstrate your love for Me by being My people."

The people said, "How can we demonstrate our love for You?"

"By keeping My Commandments."

"Which ones?"

"One of them is to take off one day in seven."

"God," they replied, "we can't do that. We won't survive."

"Trust Me and obey Me. In the obeying you will demonstrate that you really love Me, that you really are people of the covenant."

The Desecration of the Sabbath

What happens when they forget or misuse the Sabbath? As we move on in the history of Israel, we come across what Nehemiah calls "the desecration of the Sabbath." The people of Israel began to abuse this one day in seven. Scripture explains this two ways.

Lack of Interest

First, as in Nehemiah's time, people could simply use the Sabbath as a day for business as usual. Again the people of Israel had been carried away into bondage. Subsequently some were released and found their way back into the Promised Land, Nehemiah among them. When he got back to his homeland, it became clear to this leader that the people desecrated the Sabbath day. They simply treated it like any other day.

Their attitude demonstrated the people's utter lack of interest in worship. Although God had set aside the day, the Jews said, "We would rather do our work; we'd rather make money; we'd rather go and live our ordinary lives on this day than use it for the purpose for which God gave it to us."

Nehemiah found the people's clearly disobedient life-style appalling. Although they had an opportunity to keep this Commandment, they turned a blind eye to it, demonstrating that, where the rubber met the road, they preferred to do their own thing, rather than obey God. They demonstrated the shallowness of their covenant relationship with the Lord.

Meticulous Observance

In Christ's time we see an entirely different desecration of the Sabbath: The people became so obsessed with a meticulous observation of the day that they ended up desecrating it.

How could this be? Many earnest people felt much concern about keeping the Sabbath holy. They knew they should not do work on it. They knew they could demonstrate they were not working by not carrying a burden, but they needed a definition of *work* and one of *burden*. Some quite rightly said, "Oh, listen, we don't want to break the Sabbath; we know we must not do any work. But we're not sure what constitutes work and what constitutes a burden."

So the rabbis got together and dealt with these issues on a case-by-case basis. One little old lady wanted to know if she could wear her false teeth on a Sabbath, because she thought that might constitute a burden. The rabbis duly considered it and decided, yes, it was a burden, and she must not wear her false teeth on a Sabbath. "Thou shalt not wear thy false teeth on the Sabbath. Thou shalt gnash thy gums," they ruled.

The result of all these decisions was called the Mishna. They gathered all the rulings together, and people spent their lives learning them and teaching them so that everyone would know what he or she could and could not do on the Sabbath. It all came from an earnest desire to honor the Lord.

What happened? They spelled out all the rules. They got themselves in a rut. People worried about how far they could go on a Sabbath-day journey. According to the Mishna, they couldn't go farther than a certain distance. A man might say, "But I've got to go see my mother on such-and-such a Sabbath." So before the Sabbath, he'd travel a Sabbath-day's journey, find a tree, and put food under it. He'd say, "This is my home." Then he went home. On the seventh day of the week he walked a Sabbath's-day's journey to the tree, took the food, ate it, and said, "This is my home, now I can go another Sabbath day's journey."

If he had a really long journey, he would put more food under another tree and keep working it out this way. What happened to the rules and regulations designed to help people keep the spirit of the law? They became an end unto themselves. Bound up by restrictions and regulations, the people lost the whole sense of loving and honoring the Lord. When Christ came, He clearly objected to all this; in effect He told them, "You are desecrating the Sabbath."

Missing the Point

In both cases, the people began missing the point God tried to make. They lost sight either by ignoring or becoming hidebound by the rules. Now they could not play by the real ones.

Things got so bad at one point in Jewish history that on one occasion, when their enemies attacked, the people maintained, "To pick up our swords and defend ourselves would mean carrying a burden." They laid down their swords, and 1,000 of them were massacred, all because of the tight rules and regulations. God never intended this ludicrous end to His Commandment.

Clarification of the Sabbath

Jesus clarified the Sabbath by two things: His actions and His announcements.

How did He act? First, Scripture says in Luke 4:16 that on the Sabbath day He went into the synagogue as was His custom. In other words, He worshiped regularly on the Sabbath day. He clearly and carefully adhered to this requirement.

Second, Jesus healed on the Sabbath. On six occasions He had monumental run-ins with the authorities over whether or not He could heal on the Sabbath. The authorities had determined that to heal was to work, and you should not work on the Sabbath, therefore healing desecrated the Sabbath. Jesus answered in this way: He said He was fulfilling the law. He was Lord of the Sabbath, and He said the Sabbath was for man, not man for the Sabbath.

What did He mean by all that? When He said He had not

come to set the law apart, but to fulfill it, He meant that He Himself fulfilled all that the law prefigured. Because of this He was saying, "Listen, the Sabbath doesn't govern Me; I govern the Sabbath." Then He said, "On that basis, remember, man was not made for the Sabbath, but the Sabbath was made for man."

In other words, "In the Sabbath God graciously provides for human beings, giving man the opportunity for rest, refreshment, reflection, and the privilege of worship, obedience, and dependence. Don't get too locked in; don't swamp it with rules and regulations. Enjoy it as a precious gift from God." The Lord of the Sabbath had spoken.

Keeping the Sabbath

How do we keep the Sabbath? What do we do with it? If we look into our lives, we'll probably see that we simply operate on the basis of what we want to do, or we keep it on the basis of what tradition or upbringing insists we do. That's a far cry from thinking the rules through and coming to a conclusion before the Lord as to what we ought to do on the Sabbath day.

From Sabbath to Sunday

A strange thing happened in Christian history. Somehow or other we got from the Sabbath to Sunday—"the venerable day of the Son," as Constantine called it, when he legislated the first day of the week as the Lord's day.

How did we get from Sabbath to Sunday? The answer may give us a clue as to how we are to handle the Sabbath. The transitional period from the observation of the Sabbath on Saturday to the Christian celebration of Sunday has been handled differently in many ways in many parts of the world.

When Paul met with the disciples in Troas, it says they gathered together on the first day of the week and engaged in a worship service. When he wrote to the Corinthians, in the sixteenth chapter of the first book, he said that when they gathered on the first day of the week, they were to bring their offerings to the Lord. Paul makes only that one reference to the first day of the week. Scripture has relatively few of them. When we come to Revelation, John says he was in the Spirit on the Lord's day, the only use of that term in the Scripture.

From this we can see that in the very early days of the Christian church the believers who were Jewish continued to worship on the Sabbath day in the synagogue. They also met on other occasions. As the Gentiles came into the church, they had no obligation to accept the Jewish Sabbath, so apparently they began to meet on other days of the week. The big question is why the first day?

While we don't have any conclusive answers to that, we can make some inspired guesses. An obvious one is that the first day had a special quality for Christians because on that day Jesus rose from the dead. You'll also find, if you check post-resurrection appearances, that many took place on the first day of the week. If you calculate right, you can also find that Pentecost came on the first day of the week. Among scholars, some think things began to change to the first day of the week to honor the resurrection, post-resurrection appearances, and Pentecost.

Do you remember the biblical account of what happened when a conflict arose about whether Gentile believers should adhere to Jewish law? Acts 15 records that a council was called in Jerusalem. At the end, they decided the Gentiles should not follow every Jewish law, but out of respect for the Jewish people they should abstain from eating things with blood in them and adhere to one or two other minor guidelines, simply not to offend their Jewish brothers. No mention is made of observing the Sabbath day. They need not concern themselves with other restrictions.

This introduces a theological principle of great significance: The Christian church has begun to move the emphasis from the seventh day of the week to the first day of the week. When they did this, did they mean to transfer the Jewish Sabbath to another day, with all the Sabbath entailed, or were they saying, "We're done with that, and now we enter a new era, a totally different situation"?

Although that may not sound particularly significant, we need to wrestle with it and come up with some conclusions, because the way we handle the Fourth Commandment in our society will be determined by our answer. Today some Christians will support each side, some saying Sunday is the Jewish Sabbath transferred to another day, others claiming we are free from the law and in an entirely new situation.

Sabbatarians Versus Antinomians

Those who tell you they support the idea that the Jewish Sabbath has moved from the last day of the week to the first would probably agree with this statement from the Great Westminster Divines' Meeting and Assembly:

> The Lord's day ought to be so remembered . . . that they [our ordinary activities] may not be impediments to the due sanctifying of the day when it comes. The whole day is to be celebrated as holy to the Lord, both in public and private as being the Christian sabbath. To which end, it is requisite, that there be a holy cessation or resting all that day from all unnecessary labours; and an abstaining, not only from all sports and pasttimes, but also from all worldly words and thoughts. . . .

What time is vacant, between or after the solemn meetings of the congregation in public, [should] be spent in reading, meditation, repetition of sermons; especially by calling their families to an account of what they have heard, catechizing of them, holy conferences, prayer for a blessing upon the public ordinances, singing of psalms, visiting the sick, relieving the poor and such like duties of piety, charity and mercy accounting the sabbath a delight.

That's Sabbatarianism, and you'll find it in several forms today. The document I just quoted was written in England during the seventeenth century, under the Puritan influence, and it described what became the traditional British Sabbath. As a result the Lord's Day Observance Society came into being, which passed considerable legislation that Britain still adheres to today. When the Puritans came over to New England, they passed similar acts that we now commonly call the "Blue Laws."

I was brought up in a Sabbatarian home. In my childhood we went to Sunday-morning church, Sunday-afternoon church, Sunday-evening church. In between those three experiences, we played no games and could not play outside; instead we prayed or read or took part in quiet family conversations. Once my parents got a radio, they never switched it on on the Lord's day. Neither would they dream of going to a restaurant on a Sunday; that would require someone else to work.

Many earnest people are Sabbatarians. On Sunday they take no part in sports, and they believe there should be no games. People should be in the place of worship, they demur, giving the day over exclusively to the service of the Lord.

Should you be a Sabbatarian? Everyone needs to answer that question for himself. He also needs some good reasons for his answer, because he will want to take God's Word seriously.

The Antinomian approach contrasts entirely with the Sabbatarian one. An Antinomian simply disregards the law, and his response to it may take many forms. "We are not under law. We're under grace," such Christians often say. Really they mean, "Hey, listen. You know why those guys worshiped on Sunday instead of Saturday? They felt so relieved to get out from under the restrictive practices that were only a shadow of Christ's reality, His freedom, His love; they discovered that He would introduce them to the eternal Sabbath, and they were heading for eternal rest.

"When they found out about eternal rest, then they said, 'Hey, forget it. We can just be free and enjoy ourselves, relax and do whatever we wish.' " Not much theological basis for that viewpoint, but it feels good not to have to do anything, as far as these folks are concerned. You probably know at least a few Antinomians.

Now, can we make a solid case for either from Scripture? Well, it depends on which Scriptures you use, which is why this remains a major controversial issue among Christians.

Responsible Discipleship

I'd like to suggest that we neither impose Sabbatarianism nor countenance irresponsible Antinomianism. Instead we should look toward developing an attitude of responsible discipleship.

What does that mean? Paul says we don't need to let anybody judge us regarding holy days or Sabbath days, that we can worship some days as to the Lord, or we can not worship some days as to the Lord. Because we should honor the Lord *every day*, it should not be a major principle.

Now watch out! If we say, "Every day is special to the Lord," we may really end up living with no day special to the Lord. You've seen it when you've got a job a lot of people should do.

If it becomes everybody's responsibility, what happens? It ends up nobody's responsibility—and no one does it. It's the same with days declared holy to the Lord. Christians need to come to this point and say, "I rest in the Lord. I trust in the Lord. I obey the Lord—every single day of the week. In my secular employment, in my ordinary responsibilities, in the mundane things of life, I do them all as unto the Lord. Every day is a special one before Him." Then they must live that way.

In addition we have one very special day each week. God grants us that extraspecial day in order that we might use it to sharpen our focus on Him, on what it means to serve the Lord, to worship, and obey Him. In our society, that happens to be the first day of the week. We thank God for that day of the week and do not abuse it.

Not long ago, when I visited Bangladesh, I discovered the Christians there worshiped on the sixth day of the week—enough to give a Sabbatarian a heart attack! Why? Because Bangladesh is an Islamic state, so they've decreed Friday as the Sabbath. The Christians there didn't say, "Hey, listen, we're going to work on the sixth day of the week, but we won't show up for the first day of the week." They couldn't do that. Instead they said, "Lord, it's not a matter of Sabbatarianism; it's a matter of serving You every day. If the one day happens to be the sixth or the seventh or the first or the eighth or whatever, it's utterly without consequence. We will take it as it comes from You and use it for Your glory."

That seems the right approach, to me. How do we put it all together? Do you say you should do certain things on the Lord's day? I hope so. Do you have convictions about what you won't do on the Lord's day? That would seem reasonable. But do you feel free to legislate what you should and shouldn't do and to legislate the actions of others? Suppose this Sunday there's a ball game. Ought you to go? Or what if the symphony came to town then? Should you go, or shouldn't you? How do you handle these questions?

It depends on whether you're a Sabbatarian or Antinomian, or whether you've said, "Lord, I'll tell You what I'm going to do. I'm going to take Sunday as a gift from You, and I'm going to use it responsibly. At the end of the day I'll feel very happy presenting it to You and saying, 'Lord, this was Your day, and this is what I did with it.' "

If you can do that on Sunday, as you do it every other day of the week, I submit that you'll be honoring the Lord. As you honor Him in this way, you'll demonstrate something—that you're a member of His covenant—and you'll show that by loving obedience to Him.

Honor your father and your mother, so that you may live long in the land the Lord your God is giving you.

Exodus 20:12

5

Life in the Family

"Honor your father and your mother," those well-known words seem to take a lot for granted, don't they? First they presuppose that you know who your parents are. Second, they assume you know them well enough to appreciate their significance. Finally they imply that you have a situation in which you have every opportunity to honor them, pay them respect, and let them know how deeply you feel about them.

Today it's rather easy to say, "Honor your father and mother," when, if you really come down to it, I may not know my father and mother. Or I might more accurately say, "Listen, I have become so embittered against them—I am so good at blaming them for everything that's gone wrong in my life—that frankly I *don't* appreciate them." Maybe I honestly have to say, "I am so out of touch with them that there's absolutely no way I can realistically express my appreciation to them and tell them they mean much to me."

What does it take to have a situation where we can know our parents, honor them, and express appreciation for them? It requires an environment that fosters an ongoing relationship. What do we mean by an environment of this sort, one that supports deep-rooted, interwoven relationships?

We've just described a family, of course. The Fifth Commandment talks to us about what God expects in our family living.

Why Should I?

When we think about this Commandment and living in such a God-ordained environment, some might say, "Why should I honor my father and mother?" Scripture gives us some reasons, and I would point out four with little comment indeed.

First, in Exodus 20, God says to honor your parents "...so that you may live long in the land the Lord your God is giving you." In Deuteronomy 5, in the parallel passage that repeats the Commandments before the people enter the Promised Land, God gives the reason "...that it may go well with you...." In the New Testament we find Paul picking up these ideas and elaborating on them. In Colossians 3:20 he says children should obey their parents, "for this pleases the Lord." Finally, in Ephesians 6:1, he simply says you should honor them because "this is right."

Why honor your parents?

> It pleases the Lord
> It is the right thing to do
> It enables you to live long in the land
> It will be well with you

These things may not grip us too much, so let me give you another reason that's not in the Bible. In Joy Davidman's book on the Ten Commandments, called *Smoke on the Mountain*, she retells one of Grimm's fairy tales. It tells of some parents who had both children and one grandfather living with them.

Grandfather was getting a little old and sloppy. At mealtimes he tended to get his soup and porridge in places they shouldn't have gone. The parents felt concerned about this and remonstrated with granddad, but he really couldn't do anything about it.

In the end they didn't allow the old boy to sit at the table with the family anymore, but sat him in the corner of the room. Joy Davidman paints a very sad picture of this old man stuck in the corner of the room in disgrace, because he couldn't handle his food very well. Being isolated didn't help much, in fact it just allowed the situation to deteriorate until he couldn't handle his eating at all. So they made him a trough. They put his food in the trough and took away his knife, fork, and spoon; so he was made to pick up the food with his fingers and stuff it in his mouth.

The situation went from bad to worse, until one day the parents noticed the children playing in the shed. The youngsters had a saw and some wood and hammer and nails, and they seemed to be building something. The parents asked, "What are you building?" The children responded, "A trough for when you get old."

The moral of the story is, "Honor your father and mother, because one day you might want your children to do the same to you." Your children may well learn how to honor you from observing how you honored your parents.

We have five good reasons for honoring our parents, but in today's society, in which everything changes so rapidly, it has become increasingly hard to live in the kind of environment that supports these rules.

The Extended Family

First of all, the Old Testament and New Testament family is very different from the family we speak of today. If you look at our single-family dwelling, you immediately see what the twentieth-century person means by a *family*. Over the past century our single-family dwellings have gotten smaller and smaller. Why? Because the average family now has 2.4 children, the dog, and a television. That's more or less our definition of a family—we call it a "nuclear family."

The Hebrew and Greek languages don't have a word for our nuclear family; the idea is foreign to them. Each language has two words to describe *family*. In Hebrew one means "a wide-ranging network of blood relationships"; our word *clan* might best describe it. The second word in Hebrew means "a household of people." Joshua 7 best illustrates this for us. Somebody in the people of Israel has done something really bad, and they have to find out who did it. So they are told to come out in their twelve tribes. Then each of the tribes divides into clans. Then each clan divides into families, and each household is questioned individually. The word for "household" is the second Hebrew word.

The Greek language conveys the same ideas. In Luke 2 it says the parents of the Lord Jesus went down to Bethlehem for the census because Joseph was of the house and lineage of David. It describes the same ideas: the clan (or lineage); and the house (or household). The biblical family not only included the mother and father, 2.4 children, the dog, and the television, but also unmarried aunts, widowed uncles, grandfather, and grandmother—what we commonly call the extended family.

The biblical writers have this concept of family in their minds when they tell us to honor our father and mother. Why? Because parents clearly had far-reaching responsibilities for a wide variety of relationships. Through them the family provided essential services.

Economic Survival

First, the family provided economic survival. That is how I understand the expression "honor your father and your

mother, so that you may live long in the land. . . ." The Israelites were headed for inhospitable territory, where they faced
very precarious economic situations. Quite frankly, they could
only hold out by sticking together and working together for
their own support.

In primitive societies today, you find the same structure. Recently I saw a film on the Gabbra tribe of Northern Kenya. Living in the inhospitable deserts of that country, their economy
requires at least four people, working nine hours a day, seven
days a week, just to handle the flocks. That time doesn't allow
for other jobs, either. Without those four herdsmen, the tribe
could not survive.

Because of this economy, the men of the Gabbra tribe cannot
marry until after their mothers have reached the end of their
childbearing years. When a man does marry, he cannot own
any property whatsoever. Why? Because he has to work for
the family's survival.

Emotional Stability

The family also provided emotional stability. Deuteronomy
5:16 further expands this Commandment to say "Honor your
father and your mother, as the Lord your God has commanded
you, so that you may live long and that it may go well with
you. . . ." In other words, honor them so that you may have
emotional stability. Where did emotional strength come from
for the Israelites? From a household that held many opportunities for ongoing interaction and for a network of relationships.
From being part of a clan, each person gained innumerable
chances to relate to others of varying backgrounds and in-
sights.

Think of it this way. If you have two parents and four
children of the right mix, you have the possibility for eight
relationships: husband-wife, father-son, father-daughter,
mother-son, mother-daughter, brother-brother, sister-sister,

brother-sister. Think of the opportunities, even in a family that size, to learn how old folks operate and how young ones do, how boys get along with boys, how girls get along with girls, and how girls get along with men. . . . Just imagine all the combinations! It breeds emotional stability.

Add to that the uncles, aunts, and grandparents; throw in a few servants from all around the place and some aliens, all living in the same household, and what have you got? You have extended relationships that stand for the possibility of increased emotional strength. I have a theory that many people need counseling today because they have gotten away from their extended families. Some time ago the "young-timers" could get an awful lot of common-sense teaching from the old-timers. Without those extended families, they've lost that depth of experience.

If you think in terms of family, you also gain a sense of belonging, a sense of identity. Many people adopted as small children have later discovered a need to find out about their "real" parents. It happens more and more. Why? Because these children have lost their sense of identity. Once they've deeply appreciated their adopted parents, they begin to feel they've lost some kind of lineage—they've lost their roots.

Educational Structure

In addition to allowing for economic survival and emotional stability, the family performed a role as an educational structure. The Old Testament provided room for parent-child dialogue. It made the most of the child's delightful habit of asking questions. The child had a question, and a parent happened to be around. Son has a question, dad has the answer—there's the educational structure.

What happens today?

A boy says to his father, "How hot is the sun, dad?"

"I don't know, son."

"How far is it from the sun to Venus, dad?"

"I'm afraid I don't know."

"Do you know how long it would take to get to Venus from Mars, dad?"

"I really don't, son."

"You don't mind my asking these questions, dad, do you?"

"No, son. How are you going to learn if you don't ask questions?" We've lost our sense of the importance of education.

Can you see the three-pronged structure that made so much sense in the Old Testament? Somebody had to hold everything together socially. Someone had to provide economic survival, emotional stability, and educational structure. Who did? The old patriarch, with his wife, the mother, assisting. Mother and father were very honorable. You couldn't make it without them. It was as simple and basic as that.

Today's Family

Now we move into modern times and see some drastic changes. Let's just look at a few.

First we've moved from the extended family to the nuclear family. The old family homes of the last century got broken up into three or four apartments, because of smaller nuclear families. We've lost that broad basis of support.

Second, we've moved from an emphasis on hierarchy to one on individuality. Instead of looking out for the good of the family, we tend to look for the good of the individual. For instance, we send our kids out to get jobs because we say, "Work is good for you." Almost as soon as they start to work, they get their paycheck and say, "That's my money." They open their own bank accounts, buy their own cars; and parents, forget it. You have no hold over them at all.

For that reason, when our kids got jobs we insisted that we control the bank account, because they were still our children, and we were still their parents, and we wanted some sort of cohesive family living, rather than a houseful of people splitting and doing their own thing.

Third, we've changed from a sense of stability to modern mobility. We can get around quickly and can go far; we love to be on the move, and the idea of staying in a certain area and putting down roots becomes very foreign indeed. We like the idea of moving all the time. I understand people now stay in an area an average of three to four years, then they move on.

Finally we've also gone from an emphasis on the traditional to one on the novel. We tend to look down on "old-fashioned" things, seeking "alternate life-styles." We want things to continually seem fresh, new, and exciting. Over and over you hear, "That's boring." *Boring* means "unacceptable." We look for something different and turn from tradition.

What Caused These Changes?

Where do these changes come from? One cause is urbanization. In the old days people lived on the family farm or out in the deserts or they were pioneers out West. In order to survive, they had to hang together, because alone they could not survive. With the Industrial Revolution, all that went by the board. People moved from the country to great urban centers, where they discovered a chance to spread their wings, do their own thing, get away from oversight and correction. To a large extent, urbanization and industrialization destroyed the extended family.

In addition we now have a different method of communication. In the extended family, communication and data were filtered down through the hierarchy of the family, but now anyone can listen to television or the radio or put on earphones and isolate himself from the rest of the world. What he gets from such communications may not be in line with what the family stands for.

What has happened? We reap the benefits of better housing, better health, better education, better vacations, better all kinds of stuff. But are those the only consequences of change? No. We have also suffered a marked deterioration in relationships. We no longer honor parents; instead we lie on a counselor's couch and blame our parents. We don't concentrate on what they did right, but on what they did wrong.

Broken relationships become the order of the day. We have an increase in emotional disorders and people who need all kinds of help in coming to terms with emotional conflict. To a large extent this directly results from the breakdown of our built-in societal systems.

In addition we face all kinds of confusion concerning values. What is right? What is wrong? A youngster probably has a different set of beliefs from his parents'—he does things differently. As a consequence he listens to all kinds of voices and picks up on all kinds of ideas. Mother and father look at all these things and ask, "What on earth is happening?"

Where Are We Going?

Now if we think of the past—the biblical family—the present—our modern family—and look into our crystal balls toward the future, what will we see?

People have made predictions about our families' futures. The pessimistic view, voiced by a world-renowned sociologist and psychologist, says the family faces extinction. The optimistic view takes the opposite side, saying, "The turbulence of tomorrow will drive people into deeper relationships." What will happen? Only time will tell.

Alvin Toffler, in his book *Future Shock,* takes what I call a mediating view, combining both outlooks. He tells us, "The family will break up and shatter," that's the pessimistic view, "and it will then come together again in weird and novel ways," that's the optimistic view.

Toffler may be on to something here. What does he mean by the family coming together in weird and novel ways? He talks about the results of new technology and what that could offer us. Before long, we could have "embryo emporiums," he says. Parents could simply go out and buy a baby. Someone else will go through the whole messy business of having the infant for them.

Sound farfetched? Maybe not. Not long ago on television I saw a program about some cattle dealers who flew to Hawaii on a chartered plane. On the way there they had a cattle auction, 37,000 feet above sea level, the highest and biggest cattle auction in the world. "How did they get all those cattle on the plane?" you ask. They didn't, because the auction simply sold off embryos and semen. Afterwards when the interviewer asked, "What did you buy?" one man said, "Twenty semen." Another told the reporter, "Six embryos." If we have technology to do that with animals, it's only a matter of time until we have the technology to do it with humans. Once we have the technology, we feel we have the absolute right to go ahead with it.

Toffler talks about the possibility of professional parents. Many couples who have two careers do not particularly want to bother with kids. We've seen this more and more. Still, they'd like to have the advantages of children, so they'd go to a baby emporium, pay someone to have the child for them, and then send the child to professional parents, who specialize in bringing up children. The couple would reserve visitation rights through contract.

When we compare today's family to the biblical norm for a

family, once we've seen the changes that have already oc-
curred, that future possibility doesn't seem so farfetched.
We're considerably closer to that than we are to the biblical
norm.

Toffler also talks about serial marriages. When he wrote this
fourteen years ago, it didn't happen too often. It does now. Serial marriages are the norm. He just pointed out the difference
between old-style polygamy and today's marriage style, when
he said, "We have polygamy today, but serially and sequen-
tially, not contemporaneously." Under the old rules about polygamy you had a lot of wives at once; now you just have them
one after the other.

Next, he says, serial marriages produce aggregate families.
This just means, "Those are yours, and those are mine, and
these are ours together." We begin to produce "semi-siblings."

I'm not being a prophet of doom and gloom. I'm simply
projecting what sociologists and psychologists currently say.
The family today, they predict, is in all probability doomed,
and we will soon end up with all manner of different situations.

If we move farther from the old biblical norms, what on
earth will happen in the future? Can we work within the biblical principles if we don't even know our parents? Or if we do
know them, but not deeply? Or if we aren't close enough to
them to express appreciation?

As we move away, still talking about honoring our parents,
we may come out with empty platitudes, unless we begin to
take seriously the changes in our society concerning marriage
and the family. What do we need to apply this Commandment?

Unchanging Factors

Despite all the confusion in the family, some unchanging
factors remain. I want to identify three.

A Divine Origin

First the family has a divine origin. We can tinker around with "alternate life-styles" as much as we want, but we must remember that as soon as we begin to move away from structural norms for society, we increase the probability that we'll introduce uncontrollable factors. The Creator of the universe built in certain principles for its operation. For example, He included some ecological rules in its function. Today we readily recognize man as the biggest enemy of ecological balance, and as we become increasingly aware of this we endeavor to rectify the situation, to play by the rules.

What about the damage we have done to ourselves? If we may tinker with ecological norms and produce chaos, what can we do to our society? We must understand that God ordained sociological principles, too, and we move away from them at our peril.

Check the beginning of Genesis. If you read the early history of the human race, you know God was thinking *family*. Look at Adam, look at Noah, look at Abraham, look at Israel—all the time the growing, expanding family, but clearly in the structure of a divine ordinance. If you still doubt the divine plan, go to the New Testament, Ephesians 3:14, 15, where Paul says he's praying to God the Father, the Father from whom every family in heaven and earth is named.

We probably lose something in the translation here. The Greek words for *father* and for *family* are almost identical. Paul shows the inextricable link between the Father and the family, the Father in heaven and the family here on earth.

A Divine Order

Second, the family has a divine order. God clearly ordained two things: The order of the family requires that a father and mother must be honored; and the father and the mother must be honorable.

To *honor* father and mother means literally "to state one is deserving of respect, attention, and obedience." Isaiah says, "God complains that the people honor him with their lips but not with their hearts" (see Isaiah 29:13). We face the danger of honoring our parents with our lips and not our hearts.

Why should I honor my parents? Because God ordained that my father should have part in my protection, direction, and provision for my need. To a greater or lesser part, he did. He may have done a lot wrong, but what did he do right? Have I acknowledged those things? How can I honor my mother? She brought me to birth and gave me that initial care. From her I began to learn about life. If my temperament is determined by the time I reach age six, what role did my mother play in making me the person I am? If I turned out halfway decent, does she get any credit for it?

You may honor your parents in many ways. When my mother was dying of cancer in England, I felt very frustrated that I just could not get back to see her. We weren't sure how much longer she had. Among other things, at that time I was finishing the manuscript for my book *What Works When Life Doesn't?* So I chose to dedicate the book to my mother. I mailed the dedication to her, and she got it the day before she died. The last thing she read from me said:

> To Mary, my mother, who brought me to life, who taught me to work, who inspired me to preach, and who, during the preparation of this manuscript, has battled cancer with quiet courage and unshaken faith, proving once again that she knows what works when life doesn't.

You may not have such a dramatic way of expressing the honor you feel for your parents, but you need to take advantage of any opportunities you have to tell them of it.

In order to receive honor, parents also need to be honorable. In the New Testament Paul says, "Obey your parents," to the children. Then he says, "Parents, don't drive your children nuts" (that's my free translation). He means that parents have a sense of divine accountability and divine responsibility. They must take their parenting so seriously before God that others get the message, that kids will know their parents are really into being the parents God ordained them to be. Of course when the parents behave honorably, children find it easy to honor them.

A Divine Opportunity

That leads us to the third unchanging factor: the family's divine opportunity. The family has an opportunity from God to assist those beginning to consider establishing a family. We need to help young people do it His way. Today we get so much conflicting information about family life from the media that if you aren't confused, you aren't listening. The answer to that confusion comes from God Himself.

First, though, I need to offer a word of warning on this. In the church some people have become so concerned about family breakdown that they major on that to the exclusion of everything else. Others who have noticed this tendency now talk about "deification of the family" within the church.

We need some balance here. Jesus said, "Don't think I came to bring peace, I didn't. I came to bring a sword." Again He told us, "The sword that I will bring will set a mother against her daughter, a father against his son, and—believe it or not—a daughter-in-law against her mother-in-law."

What did Jesus mean? He goes on to explain, "And anybody

who loves father or mother or child more than Me is not worthy of Me." In other words, He's said, "Don't you *dare* deify the family. Don't ever make the family the number-one consideration. *I* am the number-one consideration; I am the Lord, not your kids. I am the Lord, not your family. I am the Lord, not your marriage. I will be the Lord of your children, your household, your marriage. But I will never surrender My Lordship to any or all of these things."

So if you plan to initiate a family, make sure you start off right. But what do we do for those who have already started and have done lots wrong? What about young people who look at their parents and say, "I blew it, and I've blown it all over the place." What about parents who can echo that sentiment?

Where possible we can take the opportunity to give these people a new start. Some children feel deeply hurt about their parents; they may tell us about incest in their families or of the abuse handed them by drunken fathers; others tell us of physical beatings they received from parents. All need compassionate help dealing with their hurts and pains.

One woman from halfway across the country called me to tell me her story. She had experienced an affair, divorce, and remarriage to a divorced man. Each had children by their first marriage. Recently they had come to know the Lord. "What should we do?" she wanted to know. "Should we divorce and go back to our original partners, who also are believers and have refused to remarry?"

I felt like saying, "Lady, we've got enough people with that problem here. I don't need to hear about it from halfway across the country," but I didn't. What can we do for such hurting people?

I'll tell you what we can do. Although we can't always give them a fresh start, we can help them deal with the hurts and pains of wrongdoing. We need to commit ourselves to them.

What can we do for those who have no way of putting things right? Children who cannot forgive because their parents are gone, yet they still suffer from emotional scars, resentment, and bitterness? We can remind them that they have been forgiven, if they have accepted Jesus as their Savior. Because of the forgiveness they've experienced in Him, they can begin to learn what it means to forgive in His name.

Fulfilling that divine opportunity takes the power of the Spirit, the name of Christ, and the support of the body of Christ; it takes all the resources made available to us by a gracious God to become realistically involved in what it means to be a mother or father, a grandma or grandpa, or a child or grandchild in today's society. Things have changed so drastically, we've gotten miles away from the biblical norm, and at our present rate of nonprogress, we'll end up thousands of miles away from it in the near future.

What about the society outside the church? What of those who never come to church, who don't know what the Word of God says and could care less about Jesus, His cross, and forgiveness? What about the kids on our street, contemplating marriage; or not even bothering with marriage; or taking part in trial marriages? What do we say to them? What are we showing them? How have we ministered to them?

In this whole area we must get ahold of those old-time principles and show how those unchanging rules can work, even in a changing family scene. As we do this under God we can become an untold blessing to people who need us desperately.

You shall not murder.

Exodus 20:13

6

The Sanctity
of Human Life

Most of us find the King James Version translation of the Sixth Commandment most familiar: "Thou shalt not kill." In a very straightforward statement consisting of four monosyllabic words, God confronts us with complex ideas that require our best thinking and deepest spiritual concern.

What Does it Mean to Kill?

In order to understand what this verse implies, we need to comprehend the meaning of the word translated "kill" by the scholars of King James's era. The New International Version translates the same word "murder" because these modern scholars felt it more accurately conveyed the idea of the original language. Hebrew has other words that could more accurately be translated "kill." This Commandment does not aim at prohibiting all killing as much as it prohibits taking life with forethought.

To clarify the issue, let's take a look at other verses that deal with similar subjects. Deuteronomy 20 gives the Bible's rules for war—and they certainly got into quite a few wars in the Old Testament. How can we say the Bible says "thou shalt not kill," yet gives rules for war? We can't unless we understand this chapter of Scripture as one that places severe limits on warfare. Yes, God's people could go to war, but they could not kill women and children. They could do certain things, but not destroy others.

Exodus 21:12, 13 gives minute descriptions concerning murderers and how they should be handled. Quite clearly Scripture distinguishes between those who kill accidentally and those who kill on the basis of premeditation: Anyone who killed on purpose received capital punishment, while those who took another's life unintentionally received a different treatment. The distinction related to motive.

To care for those who killed without forethought, Numbers 35 institutes the cities of refuge. In those days if somebody had killed someone else, the police didn't come to his door, because they didn't have police; and they didn't take each other to the law courts and get lawyers and so on. If one person intentionally killed another, the relatives of the victim killed the guilty party. That was it. But sometimes, without vengeance or hatred, one man would slay another accidentally. In such a case the killer would go to a city of refuge, before anyone caught him.

The city of refuge gave the killer a place to stay while others carefully looked up the facts, checked his motivations, and began the proper judicial procedures. Such cities were provided to show that the people of God differentiated between vengeful, malicious killing and accidental manslaughter. They also showed that while it was legitimate for the families of those who were murdered to kill the killer, there was no place for vigilante-style mayhem.

In the Image of God

What rationale lies behind "Thou shalt not kill"? Genesis 9:6 describes the prohibition against malicious, premeditated slay-ing when it says, "Whoever sheds the blood of man, by man shall his blood be shed. . . ." We call this Old Testament system *lex talionis,* "the law of retaliation." It didn't mean that if somebody did this to you, you *had* to do the same to him, as people often misinterpret "an eye for an eye, and a tooth for a tooth." No, the system meant, if you take somebody else's eye, the punishment meted out to you cannot *exceed* the taking of your eye. The law limited the retaliation.

In the same way Genesis 9:6 provides limitation. If somebody sheds another person's blood, that first person's blood must also be shed. And the verse gives the reason: ". . . for in the image of God has God made man."

As we talk rather lightly about the sanctity of human life, let's ask ourselves, *What makes human life so sacred? What's the big deal?* We can answer, *Because man is made in the image and in the likeness of God.*

What does that mean? Some people would try to tell us that man is a highly developed animal. Well, we would have to agree with that. When we look around at other animals, it becomes obvious man is the most highly developed. Some folks have a problem with this idea, yet for the life of me I can't think why. Recently a little girl had a baboon heart placed in her, and she lived for some time. Obviously some degree of compatibility exists between an animal heart and a human body.

We all know doctors carry out experiments for medication and surgery on animals before they try them on humans. Why? Because a similarity exists between us. Before men went into space, scientists sent up animals, to check their reactions, which would simulate ours in many ways. We don't need to argue that man is a highly developed member of the animal kingdom. We know that.

If someone says, "Man is *only* an animal," we need to argue. That statement makes it hard to support the sanctity of human life. We would reply, "Man *is* a highly developed animal, but God has also made man in His image."

What does that mean? If you ask, you'll discover various people have different ideas. For instance, some say man alone, of all the animal kingdom, is capable of conceptual thought: He can come up with ideas; he can take data and compare it with other data; he has imagination, can be creative and artistic; he can produce all kinds of things. These abilities put him in a different league from the other animals.

In addition man can cooperate with the divine creative purpose. From God he has received both the mandate for the responsibility for the care and well-being of creation and moral sensitivity. About morality Mark Twain quipped: "Man is the only animal that blushes and has reason to." Truly man has a sense of what's right and wrong, what's fair and unfair, what's just and unjust. Does any other part of the animal kingdom have such abilities?

Finally man has the ability to communicate with God and to be communicated to by Him. This is a major distinctive and characteristic of his uniqueness. This communication potential will find its fulfillment in eternity, when the redeemed will share God's glory and worship Him forever. Mankind has an eternal dimension.

Challenging Divine Intention

Accordingly when we think about the destruction—out of vengeance or malice, on a premeditated basis—of that which God has made in His image, we recognize we deal with a subject of tremendous importance and concern. Why? Destruction of that made in the image of God challenges the divine intention. If God makes man for eternity and gives him the ability to function in relationship to Him, anyone who kills that man destroys what God had in mind. The destroyer shakes his fist in the face of God.

Murder abrogates divine authority. If divine authority holds man in this world for a time, then takes him into eternity, the man stepping in and terminating that existence on earth tries to take the place of God. Ending human life means despising the divine evaluation. God says He has made man in His image, therefore man has profound significance. Taking that life says, "I disagree, God. This person's life does not have enough significance to deserve maintaining it."

Someone has put it this way: "Man is God in effigy." We all know the anger we feel when someone gets some straw, stuffs it in an old suit, ties up the legs and arms, puts a placard on it saying, "This is Ronald Reagan," hangs it on a pole, and burns it. Why do we feel upset? It's only straw, an old suit, and a pole. We get upset because that effigy speaks of the person it stands for. The actions insult the man behind the effigy.

If man is God in effigy, when we destroy man, we insult God. For that reason God prohibits the premeditated, vengeful killing of that made in His image.

What's the Practical Relevance?

What practical relevance does the Sixth Commandment have for us today? I want to identify four areas in which that particular law has deep influence on us at this time in human history.

Abortion

What does "thou shalt not kill" have to say on abortion? What's the nature of the abortion issue?

In 1973, following the lead of the USSR and the United Kingdom, the United States passed legislation that gave a woman the right to an abortion. The lawmakers did not base that decision on the consideration of the rights of the unborn, but on the rights of the individual. Basically they thought, *A woman is an individual. She has her rights, including the right to privacy. What is more private than her body? Therefore nobody has a right to interfere with what a woman does with her body.* Sounds logical, sounds very reasonable. The Supreme Court agreed to that statement, and enacted the law.

As a result, in the United States of America today, we have 3 abortions every minute, which adds up to 4,000 abortions every day. This means that since 1973 we can estimate that 15 million abortions have been performed in our country alone. Since the Bible states that human life is sacred, and we live in a society that quite calmly destroys 15 million unborn children, we need to ask ourselves, *Is this right or wrong? Is this acceptable?*

You've probably noticed that abortion becomes a highly emotional issue, that people bomb the clinics where abortions take place, that they picket places where people go for abortion counseling. Some write to those whose children have had abortions, and all kinds of things are happening where people bring pressure to bear upon doctors who perform abortions. Meanwhile, on the other side, people level all kinds of charges. In the abortion issue we have a highly publicized, highly personal, but totally social question. As an issue, it's a real doozy! We can easily get caught up in it from various points of view. A Christian needs to look at how the Sixth Commandment applies to the abortion issue in our society today.

First let's clarify what the Supreme Court did and did not say. The court said a woman has a right to an abortion, because of the privacy of her own body, but it is not an absolute right. In her first trimester, she has a right to abortion on demand, period. In the second trimester, that right remains, but the state can make some regulations concerning the procedures. In the third trimester the state can, if it wishes, bar abortions, except when the mother's life is in some way jeopardized. So abortion is a right, but not one so broad you could drive a tank through it.

Now then if the Sixth Commandment categorically forbids us to destroy that which is made in the image of God, is that child in the womb something made in His image? If so, then abortion is horrendously wrong.

What status should we confer upon the fetus? If you look to the Bible for answers, you'll find some interesting statements. For instance Exodus 21:22 talks about a situation in which two men fight and cause a woman to give birth prematurely, but she suffers no serious injury. The offender, Scripture says, must be fined whatever the husband demands and the court allows. People have interpreted this in various ways.

Some say that it means that if, through the men's struggling, she accidentally miscarries, no suggestion is made that the life of the offender should be laid down on the basis of blood for blood and life for life. Those arguing this way claim it means that Scripture does not consider the fetus a human being, because if it did, it would demand the life rather than the fine.

If you move into Jeremiah 1:4, 5, however, you read a passage that describes the prophet's experience. He says: "The word of the Lord came to me, saying, 'Before I formed you in the womb I knew you, before you were born I set you apart; I appointed you as a prophet to the nations.'" God doesn't describe Jeremiah as an accident in the womb; He formed him in the womb and knew him before birth. Even before Jeremiah's birth, God had set him apart as a prophet.

Psalms 139:13–16 makes some powerful statements, too. "For you created my inmost being; you knit me together in my mother's womb. I praise you because I am fearfully and wonderfully made; your works are wonderful. . . . My frame was not hidden from you when I was made in the secret place. When I was woven together in the depths of the earth, your eyes saw my unformed body. All the days ordained for me were written in your book before one of them came to be."

As we move into the New Testament, we discover the lovely story of Mary, told she will bear the Messiah and going to see the already pregnant Elizabeth. When Mary makes the announcement, the unborn John the Baptist leaps in Elizabeth's womb; he recognizes what is going on.

The Bible certainly says the unborn one is capable of relationships, of some sort of spiritual insight, and of receiving some sort of divine purpose. It specifically states that God forms it. Some people therefore say that which is in the womb is from the moment of conception made by God and under the principle of the Sixth Commandment. Under no circumstances at all must we touch it.

Having said that, we need to look at the medical information available to us. Physicians have given us a wide variety of suggestions about when the fetus becomes human. Let me draw seven of them (outlined by Oliver O'Donavan and quoted in Norman Anderson's *Issues of Life and Death*) to your attention.

1. The first group would say the fetus becomes fully human at the point of conception. Among those some would say "the point of conception" rather unguardedly, while others would describe it not as a moment, but a process that we cannot accurately measure. But both would agree that, whenever it takes place, the child becomes invested with the divine image.

2. Others would say that the problem with the first theory is that 50 percent of all impregnated ova disappear in the natural course of events. If that is the case, then 50 percent

of unborn, unformed, unimplanted ova have the divine image and simply drift off into eternity without having existed in any meaningful sense at all. These people state that the person starts to be formed at implantation; before that it has no meaningful existence at all.

3. A third set says the fetus becomes human when it takes human shape. They say it will measure at least three centimeters, which will happen between forty-five and forty-nine days after conception.

4. Still another group would say it becomes human at animation. Old-time theologians used to try to figure out when the body got the soul and when the soul left. They thought of the body having a soul, as opposed to thinking that we are body, soul, and spirit. When it came to animation, people believed—and in some circumstances still do believe—that a time exists when the fetus becomes ensouled. To give you an idea how things have changed, Aristotle said that took place twenty-five to forty days after conception for the male, but fifty to eighty days after conception for the female.

5. A fifth way of thinking says the fetus becomes human at viability—the point at which it could survive without its mother. We have a problem with this today because, with our rapidly advancing technology the fetus's viability point changes all the time. Supreme Court Justice Sandra Day O'Connor said, "Fetal viability in the first trimester of pregnancy may be possible in the not too distant future." If that happens, it will make the Supreme Court's ruling palpable nonsense. So the problem then becomes that it just depends on which doctor you ask at what time and where technology has gotten to.

6. Another set of people would try to get the problem out of the way by simply declaring the fetus human at birth, not

before. If so, how do you take into account the biblical passages we've considered?

7. Finally some would claim that the fetus becomes fully human one year after birth. They say that at this stage the human child is comparable to all other animals at moment of birth, because human children are much more helpless than other animals.

Where will all this leave us? In a great, big fog—because when we look at Scripture, medical science, and our knowledge, we find it very difficult to pinpoint the moment the unborn becomes a human made in the image of God.

Because of this difficulty, people argue about whether the fetus is a person, is fully human, is subhuman, or is potentially human. Those in favor of aborting call it subhuman. They would compare it to an appendix—simply a pile of tissue. It lacks importance. In the light of Scripture, we cannot accept this position under any circumstances. But where are we then?

Despite the complexity of the issue and the degree of uncertainty that surrounds it, if we allow the fetus to go full term, it will become a human being. Therefore under no circumstances should we feel comfortable in agreeing to any callous or careless interference with that. If I cannot categorically say *when* something is made in God's image, I'm not even going to get close to tampering with it. It would seem we at least need to take that minimal position.

Some people may want stronger positions, and I understand that. They must also realize that if we are in favor of life, we must not only favor the life of the unborn, but also that of the mother. We need to express concern for the mother, her physical well-being, her emotional situation, and her spiritual state.

We need to care for the young woman whom we tell, "In having an abortion, you murdered something made in the image of God." What will that do to her emotions? How does that affect her spiritually? How can she look the world in the face again?

If we aggressively go after women who have had abortions, we may well drive them to the point of emotional breakdown or even suicide. Among those who have experienced abortions, there exists a high incidence of depression and an increasingly high level of suicide. It seems to me that if we call ourselves prolife, we must be prolife for the unborn and the born as well. We've got to be for the fetus *and* the mother, which complicates things quite dramatically.

In some cases that means we must balance out the rights of the unborn against those of the living. The Roman Catholics have arrived at a very simple answer for this: They see the rights of the fetus as the primary ones. Those in the feminist tradition and with more liberal thinking would call that nonsense, saying the rights of the living are far more important than the rights of the potentially living. How about others, who grapple with the Word of God and ask, "How do we put these together"? We need to say one or two things about this issue.

Can we countenance abortion on demand? Emphatically no! Can we ban abortion, period, for all circumstances and conditions? It would seem to me that by doing so we could get ourselves in situations where we cannot adequately deal with the needs for the life of the mother and the life of the unborn. Some people would probably agree that if the mother has a very major medical problem, and carrying the child threatens her life, action needs to be taken. To balance this out, let me quote a British physician: "In forty years of gynecological and obstetric practice, I can only remember a handful of occasions in which the mother's life was in danger because of the birth of the fetus." We need to bear that in mind.

Can we uphold the sanctity of life for both the born and the unborn? I believe we must take that position. If we wish to take a stand for the rights of the unborn, to stand against the destruction of something minimally, potentially made in the image of God, are we ready at the same time to care for those who have gone through with an abortion and feel depression, overwhelming guilt, and who might commit suicide? We need compassion for both. When we persuade women not to abort the unborn, we should help with the steps of the pregnancy that follow. But we also need to aid those who need forgiveness—we must help human lives in many dimensions, not only in the right to be born.

Suicide

Today we have a major problem with suicide among young people. It is estimated that 5,000 young people commit it every year, in the United States of America—a 300 percent increase since 1960.

People have various outlooks on suicide. We all know of the heroic approach of the Japanese kamikaze pilot. Then we've seen the Romeo and Juliet romantic view, where young lovers can't marry, but can't bear to be apart, so they end it all together. Then there's the pessimistic approach, which comes from the depths of depression, particularly with young people who lack an adequate support system to deal with that emotion.

What can we say of the person who commits suicide? Do we agree with the ancient church that would take a suicide and refuse to give him a Christian burial, refuse to bury him in a Christian graveyard? Do we say that the Bible says "thou shalt not kill," and you did the worst kind of killing—yourself? It doesn't seem we could take that kind of position.

On the other hand, do we simply shrug our shoulders and say, "It doesn't matter. If you want to commit suicide, go ahead"? Of course not, because there is something heinously wrong about suicide. It usurps divine prerogative, destroying something of intrinsic worth. In commiting suicide, a person also says to humanity, "I think you are not worth being a part of." As G. K. Chesterton said, "Suicide is the refusal to take an interest in existence; it insults everything on earth."

We've got to take a strong stand on the suicide issue. We need to make a statement that destroying that which is made in the divine image—particularly yourself—is fundamentally wrong. Having said that, do we caringly go to suicidal people, asking, "But why don't you have that support system? What happened to your family? What drove you to this depression? What can we do to assist you in this situation? How can we help you bear the burden of your trauma, even though you find yourself without the proper support system?"

In other words, if we're for the sanctity of life, let's make sure we don't just make the negative statement, "Thou shalt not kill," but that we also make a positive statement by a tremendous reaching out to those in all kinds of circumstances.

Capital Punishment

What about capital punishment? If you check in your Bible, it would appear that the Bible accepts it as a normative approach. Genesis 9:6 clearly states that whosoever sheds the blood of man, by man shall his blood be shed. Why? Because man is made in the image of God. That verse has a clear statement in it.

Today many people appeal to the Old Testament, saying Scripture requires capital punishment. Further, they tell us, the punishment fits the crime: If somebody takes it into his hands to destroy something made in the image of God, we can only demonstrate the seriousness of the act by making him pay the supreme penalty—his life.

Moreover, claim the capital-punishment advocates, we need

deterrents; if we take the life of every murderer, the rest of society will know they'd better not do it. Society needs protection from such people, they remind us, and if we get rid of them, we're certainly protected from them.

People concerned about criminals agree a punitive aspect must exist—we need a deterrent and society needs protection. However, "Shouldn't steps also be taken for the remedy of the criminal, for a restoration to some degree of normalcy?" they ask. "How can that take place if you destroy the person through capital punishment?"

Some respond that the time between the sentence and the execution allows for restoration. One wit put it this way: "One good thing about capital punishment—about the death sentence—is it wonderfully focuses the attention." These people would point to those on death row who have gotten their acts together before they were executed.

Though we may call for this Old Testament principle, today, we do not apply it across the board. The Old Testament prescribed capital punishment not only for murderers, but also for homosexuals—and for unruly teenagers. That's how you handled your delinquency problems back then—you killed them. So if we argue for capital punishment, on what grounds do we decide where it applies and where it doesn't? Do we execute blasphemers? Do we execute homosexuals? Do we execute juvenile delinquents? No, we execute murderers. If we go ahead and apply capital punishment, is this not an uneven application?

We can also easily recognize how open capital punishment is to abuse. For instance, of all those people tried for murder, 80 percent of the blacks received convictions, compared to 60 percent of the whites. Is this blind justice? Not only do we face the possibilities of error and bias, we open ourselves to the possibility of the callousing of society when we apply the death sentence. Such punishment certainly brutalizes the people involved in the execution.

Recently I saw an example of this in the story of an elderly lady executed in North Carolina. A very dear friend of mine visited this woman—the first to be executed in many years in the United States—while she was on death row. They became firm friends. The woman on death row had become a believer and had a prisonwide ministry. Although many others made appeals on her behalf, the governor of the state did not pardon her.

As the execution date neared, the prisoner became more apprehensive. My friend asked, "Would it help you in any way if I were present at your execution?" The woman welcomed what she felt would be a tremendous help to her, knowing that my friend was there praying for her at that moment and said yes.

My friend went and witnessed the execution. Five days afterwards she called me to say, "I have gone through the most excruciating thing imaginable. I can't think straight. I can't sleep. The execution keeps replaying in my mind like a bad dream. I feel I am on the verge of coming apart. Please help me."

My friend is one of the most godly, most gifted, most capable people I know—one in fact, who supports capital punishment. But she found it exceptionally difficult to witness an execution.

As far as I'm concerned, if I am in favor of capital punishment, presumably I'm in favor of doing it. How can I be in favor of it, yet say, "I wouldn't do it myself, but you do it"? If I'm not in favor of doing it myself—which I'm not—why not? It's because I have an uneasiness about it. Maybe I have that sense of unsureness because I wonder if I can be so right before God that I can clearly and absolutely know everything that went into this and feel free to take that life. I don't ever think I could arrive at that position. Could you?

War

Last we have the war issue. How do you handle the Christian's duty concerning getting into war and killing people? An activist approach says, "If the government says I've got to do it—I have to defend the shores of my homeland—then I'll do it. And I'll do it under any circumstances."

The pacifist positions vary, but many of them say, "The Lord Jesus said we should not retaliate, that those who live by the sword will perish by the sword. I absolutely cannot justify it. The way to handle things is the way of the cross, and I would rather die than make someone else die."

In between lies the selectivist approach: "Under some circumstances war is justified, and when that is the case, I will feel I can participate."

Saint Augustine introduced the idea of a just war. This doctrine has been in vogue down through the years. If you were raised in the thirties in England, as I was, you knew the meaning of a just war. It was beating Hitler and the Nazis. No problem with that. Everybody felt very patriotic and marched off—they couldn't wait to get into uniform and have a go at the Hun. It worked that way in those days.

As time went on, though, we discovered that we had bombed Dresden, which had no military value whatsoever, and we wiped it out. Then we found out we had bombed Hamburg, obliterating thousands of civilians. We justified it as retaliation for the bombings of London and Coventry. But some of us began to ask, "Where's the justice in all this? Isn't it getting out of hand?"

When America dropped the atom bomb on Hiroshima, we became even more concerned. In just a flash the explosion ushered more than 70,000 people into eternity. When the statistics came out, we noticed that as a result of World War II, in

Europe alone, 20 million Russians lost their lives. Six million Jews were exterminated; 6.5 million Germans lost their lives; 1 million Allies died. Many of us began to ask: "What is this just war?" Can we really justify more than 30 million people in Europe alone being exterminated like that? Were there things so important that they justified the taking of lives made in the image of God?

Many people began to ask some hard questions—ones that got even harder when Vietnam came along. In that conflict 4 million Vietnamese lost their lives; about 58,000 Americans lost their lives. We began to ask, "What is the justice? Where is the rightness in this thing?" People became much more concerned about war.

What's happening now? We've moved away from the war concept, into nuclear buildup. On this earth we have the equivalent of four tons of TNT for every man, woman, and child alive. If you thought Hiroshima was bad, let me tell you about the Poseidon submarine, which has sixteen missiles on board, every one with ten warheads. Every Poseidon submarine now targets 160 Soviet cities, and each warhead has the capability of three times the power of the Hiroshima bomb.

If we want we can talk about just wars, but now we confront a situation where we have the ability to destroy that over which God has made us stewards. We must ask ourselves, *In this situation do I have the freedom to move along with my society, or do I stand against it? Do I believe some principles that come from Scripture, which are so profound that I must wrestle with them—what they mean and how they apply?*

As we begin to do that, we may engage in some really hard thinking about war, capital punishment, euthanasia, suicide, infanticide, abortion, and all the other life-and-death issues. We've got to seriously apply the Ten Commandments to our day.

People don't really want to wrestle with these issues. In my church's study center we ran a course on Christian ethics, and hardly anyone applied. It seems to me that how the Sixth Commandment applies to believers today should trouble our minds.

Remember, when the Lord Jesus picked up on this issue in the Sermon on the Mount, He said, "Listen, if you kill somebody, they'll hold you before the Sanhedrin for judgment. But I'll tell you something worse than that. If you hate someone in your heart, if you're malicious, if you insult people, if you wish them dead, if you want them out of the way, if you say they're worthless, if you deny that they are what God says they are, you're not in danger of the Sanhedrin; you're in danger of hell itself."

Jesus escalated the whole thing and pinpointed the problem, which lies in our hearts. Every single one of us is capable of bitterness and hatred, of selfishness. As we begin to look at our own hearts, we might become concerned about the possibilities there.

Overcoming Evil

What rules of thumb can we apply to dealing with this issue? Read Romans 12:9, "... Hate what is evil. ..." Is there anything evil in the war issue, the capital punishment issue, the abortion issue? Well, don't just sit there and chew your gum—hate it!

If you hate evil, seek to overcome it. Don't stand by, uninvolved, but be careful, "Do not repay anyone evil for evil ..." (Romans 12:17). If we handle evil with evil, we simply compound it. Romans 12:9 continues "... cling to what is good." We need to handle evil with good. How do we handle nuclear proliferation? Not with more evil. Do we handle the abortion issue by bombing clinics? No. We need to recognize that evil has to be hated, but we must overcome it with good.

Does that seem naive in light of today's complex political situations? Not really.

In Romans 13 Paul simply and straightforwardly describes the government's role in this: It's there to reward those who do good and punish those who do evil. But what happens when government fails to do the task God appointed it to accomplish? How do we react when the government does evil? We hate it. We stand against it. And we seek to overcome it with good.

What happens if evil leaders refuse to turn around and take the side of good? Do we sit by and say, "It's my country, right or wrong"? Or can we respond, "There's no way we're going to sit idly by and let that happen"? Because we understand the sanctity of human life and know that God made us in His image, I hope we can stand up for what we believe. We can't afford to feel differently about humanity from the way God feels about it.

As we consider the meaning of the destruction of life made in God's image, as we face the issues of abortion, suicide, capital punishment, and war and seek to do something about them in our world, "thou shalt not kill" will require a great work of grace in our hearts. Before we may put the Commandment into operation, we must turn to God for forgiveness, deep love, and for the power to confront evil with good to change our world.

As God told the Israelites to live by the Commandments to show their love for Him, so He tells us to do. "If you love Me," He calls, "obey My Commandments."

You shall not commit adultery.

Exodus 20:14

7

Preserving the Sanctity of Marriage

Often people will tell you they feel turned off by the Ten Commandments. "All those 'thou shalt nots,' " they complain. "Who wants to hear that?" We all share that emotion to some degree. As soon as somebody says, "You shall not," something inside us cries, "*Oh, yes, I shall!*"

The other day I saw a sign that said DO NOT ENTER. First I thought, *Why should they say,* DO NOT ENTER? *I think I'm going to enter there.* Why did I react that way? Because I didn't like the negativism of the sign. So I decided, *If I want to go in there, I'll go—and nobody will tell me I can't!*

As I read a little farther on the sign I saw the word EXPLOSIVES. Then I realized they had a good reason for the negativism. Behind that sign lay the positive message "we are concerned for you." Now if they had put up a sign that said WE CARE FOR YOU. WE FEEL DEEPLY CONCERNED FOR YOUR LIFE. AND SOME CHEMICALS IN THIS PLACE, UNDER CERTAIN CIRCUMSTANCES, COULD CAUSE AN EXPLOSION THAT MIGHT INFLICT SOME DAMAGE ON YOUR BODY, I wouldn't have bothered to read all that. Instead they got my attention: DO NOT ENTER. Underneath they explained, EXPLOSIVES, and I immediately understood their positive concern.

The Problem of Adultery

We react the same way to the Ten Commandments. "Thou shalt not commit adultery" (KJV) sure gets your attention, doesn't it? But it seems so negative that we don't much like it. However, just as in the case of that sign, we have to realize that a positive statement lies behind the negative one. The Seventh Commandment shows God's deep concern for the sanctity of marriage. Nothing could destroy a marriage—that beautiful thing ordained by Him—more quickly than adultery. So God says, "Thou shalt not," with a positive intention.

Twentieth century Christians aren't the only ones who have problems with this Commandment. As we look in Scripture we quickly learn that the ancient cultures had problems with sexual immorality. Among the prophets, Jeremiah hit out at adulterous relationships with attention-getting words that described his contemporaries as stallions neighing after their neighbors' wives. The apostle Paul, ministering to the Corinthian church, complained, "There's an unspeakable thing going on in Corinth—you've got sexual immorality so gross I don't even want to talk about it. Yet you folks not only condone that sin, you pride yourselves on being a great church!" Obviously nobody cared about the fact that the whole Corinthian society had become permeated with sexual laxity, which had infiltrated the church.

When the Lord Jesus ministered, He talked about adultery in unexpected terms. He said, "If you lust after somebody, that's like committing adultery in your heart." In addition He described the flippant approach to divorce, so common in His day, as simply legalized adultery.

116

The Lord Jesus, the apostles, and the prophets all hit out at the insidious, pervasive problem of sexual immorality. God spoke through them because He felt concern that marriage, His fundamental structure of society, was coming apart at the seams.

What about our day and age? What can we say about our society and culture? Some people tell us we live in the greatest society on earth today; others will claim it's the greatest thing that ever happened. Frankly, I don't know where they're looking. Because if we look honestly at our society, comparing it to the ancient cultures, which fractured and fragmented, we see that we face the same danger. To combat that, we've got to consider what God says in His concern for preserving marriage.

The Curse of Adultery

Why do I call adultery a curse? I can give you six good answers to that question.

Defying God

First, adultery defies God. He says, "Thou shalt not commit adultery" (KJV). Every time a person commits this sin, he or she openly goes against what God says.

Remember the story of Joseph, who lived down in Egypt and worked for a gentleman named Potiphar? Potiphar went traveling, and while he was gone, he entrusted his house and business to young Joseph. Repeatedly Mrs. Potiphar had tried to seduce Joseph, but the young man always resisted. One day while her husband was away, she tricked Joseph into a compromising position and suggested they engage in an adulterous act. He answered, "Your husband has committed everything into my care. He entrusted it all to me. How could I abuse that trust?" Then he went a step farther, "How can I abuse that trust and sin against God?" (See Genesis 39:8, 9.)

King David got himself in a compromising situation and responded differently. He finished up committing adultery and all kinds of other terrible things. When Nathan the prophet confronted and challenged the king, David repented. Turning from the adulterous relationship with Bathsheba, in Psalm 51 he says to God: "Against You, You only have I sinned. And You are absolutely just and right in judging me" (see v. 4).

Both David and Joseph finally understood that adultery fundamentally defies God. That in itself ought to be enough for us, but being what we are, we need to know other reasons why adultery is a curse.

Destroying Families

Second, adultery destroys families. God has a commitment to the family. When He reiterates the law in Deuteronomy 6, immediately prior to the children of Israel's leaving the wilderness and entering the Promised Land, He does so in the context of the family. He says, "I have given you these laws and these Commandments and these decrees for you, your children, and your children's children" (see v. 7).

God gave the law in the context of a healthy family. From the very beginning He expressed His concern for the reproduction of human life through the family; He clearly stated that marriage and family are His way of doing things.

Now adultery destroys the sacredness, uniqueness, and specialness of marriage, the basis upon which one builds the family. Recently a woman wrote to tell me of the troubles adultery had brought to her family. Because she and her husband had taken a strong stance against their son's relationship with a married woman, they had lost the affection of all their children. The others had sided with him, against the parents' acceptance of God's Word about this sin.

As a result of their son's adultery, this couple experienced great anguish; they saw their family fall apart before their eyes. Unless we want such situations to become even more common than they are today, we have to agree with God, because if we don't say what He does about adultery, we're dead wrong. Our society shows it.

Defiling Marriage

Third, adultery defiles marriage. From the beginning God made it clear that when a man and woman come together, He makes them one. If two people come together, joined by God, publicly making a covenant and commitment to each other, then and only then do they have the freedom under God to consummate that union. They demonstrate their oneness by becoming one flesh. In simple terms it means that when two bodies come together in sexual union, that in itself is the pinnacle of their joining together by God. To consummate a union that is no union is a lie. To consummate it before it's a union is a sham. For that reason we must insist on the wrongness of sex outside of marriage. We must stand unequivocally at this point.

Now if two people marry, and one decides to take his or her sexual union outside that relationship, that person defiles what God has joined together. Over and over in the marriage ceremony we stress the commitment God requires: "Wilt thou have this woman [this man] to be thy wedded wife [husband], to live together according to God's ordinance in the holy state of matrimony? . . . Wilt thou love her [him], comfort her [him], honor and keep her [him] in sickness and in health? . . . And forsaking all others, keep thee only unto her [him] so long as you both shall live?" The answer to each is "I will."

If one of the couple does not answer, we have no marriage. Anyone who has married therefore has to understand that he or she has made a solemn covenant in the presence of God, which has joined them together. Only then may they consummate that union by sexual activity. To do so outside the marriage bond defiles the concept of marriage itself.

Denying Love

Fourth, adultery denies love. People in our modern generation will tell us that they engage in affairs because they love each other. Now who outside the relationship can dispute that? Certainly they must share some degree of affection, unless it's a one-night stand. An ongoing relationship presumably contains some kind of love, but love comes in many shapes and forms.

New Testament Greek has three words to describe love. *Eros* means "erotic love." *Phileo* describes the love of companionship. *Agape* indicates the love of commitment, love that says, "I'm primarily concerned with your well-being."

Now people can surely get into an adulterous relationship where they share marvelous *eros*. Others may get into one where the companionship is better than what they get at home. But these people do not love each other as they should before God, for one simple reason. If two people love each other with *agape* love, a total commitment to each other's well-being envelops and enriches them.

To put it more bluntly, suppose as a pastor, I engaged in an adulterous relationship with one of the ladies of my fellowship. People in the congregation came and questioned us about it, saying to me, "Stuart, you shouldn't do this. It is not right. We can't have it."

"But we love each other, and love is of God," I might reply. "The Commandments say that we should love one another."

How could my congregation respond? Could they tell me we did not love each other? Quite possibly we could share an erotic attraction. Companionship and compatibility could exist. But we could not share *agape*, because *agape* is a commitment to what God says and to the well-being of that other person. If that lady had a husband, how could I feel concern for her well-being yet fracture her marriage and take her away from her children? What on earth could I say about my wife, Jill, and my children? If I am really loving, I am primarily concerned with their good, not my own.

When people in adulterous relationships say, "We love each other," they probably do at a superficial level, but they cannot say, "We love each other in the sense God has ordained we should truly love." Adultery cannot show you're primarily concerned for others—it denies love as it really is.

Deriding Faithfulness

Fifth, adultery derides faithfulness. God has leaned out of heaven and agreed to be our God and invited us to become His people on the basis of a covenant, the essence of which is faithfulness. God says, "I will be faithful to you, be faithful to Me. Demonstrate that faithfulness by dealing faithfully with others according to My instructions."

The Old Testament writers used the same concept of covenant to hit at us with great force. Proverbs 2:17 talks about the woman who seduces a man as follows, "[She] has left the partner of her youth and ignored the covenant she made before God." If I engage in adultery, faithfulness to my wife and God has fled.

As soon as someone has shown he can be unfaithful in one area, he has shown he can become unfaithful everywhere. If we want to stand for reliability, faithfulness, and commitment, we may best do that by proving those qualities in our marriages and remaining true to our vows. As we do that we may see it beginning to spread.

Degrading People

Sixth, adultery degrades people. Romans 1:24 tells us that because of the attitude of the wicked, God has just let them go all the way into all kinds of sexual immorality and impurity. As a result, they have degraded their own bodies. We're all painfully aware of this tendency today.

Adultery can cause terrible physical damage. Not long ago the *Chicago Tribune* had a long article on the AIDS epidemic, quoting statistics projecting what may happen. Lots of people sit back comfortably and say, "Well, AIDS is just a homosexual disease, it couldn't happen to me." According to this article, shortly we may expect the disease to spread into heterosexual relationships because of today's rampant sexual promiscuity, and more recent research has proven this is now happening.

In addition adultery spreads venereal disease. Now we no longer have only gonorrhea and syphilis to contend with; scientists estimate a new venereal disease, chlamydia, may infect up to 10 million new people this year.

Not only do adulterous relationships expose people to physical damage, they also take a heavy emotional toll. To give yourself in the fullest possible way and to discover that you've been taken for a ride causes emotional scarring. Discovering your spouse has betrayed you and your vows shatters your psyche.

What then of the communal impact of adultery? One eminent historian recently concluded a study of the rise and fall of civilizations. About his research he said, "After a study of eighty-eight civilizations, I have come to the conclusion that a human society is free to choose either to display great energy or to enjoy sexual freedom. The evidence is that they cannot do both for more than one generation."

In other words, tell American society it has a choice: Engage in sexual freedom, or expend energy that will produce a superlative community. We can't do both. If we continue in the way we're going, we may have to accept that our society faces the direst of dangers. Adultery degrades people—physically, emotionally, communally, culturally, and spiritually.

The apostle Paul puts it this way: "Your body is the temple of the Holy Spirit, and how can you take that and join it in unfaithfulness?" (see 1 Corinthians 6:19). How can you take the unique property of God and engage in actions that of their very selves are the antithesis of all He stands for?

Causes of Adultery

In standing against adultery, I do not mean to sound insensitive—adultery does have causes that come from deep problems, of which I can outline four.

Uncertain Standards

First, uncertain standards open the door to adultery. Whether or not we know it, we act on the basis of what we believe. Our philosophy forms the basis of our life-style. If we know what we believe, we will know what we should do. When we have doubts about our beliefs, we feel uncertain about how we should act.

God realizes we all need some rules to play by, and He gives them to us. In the area of sexuality, He states two quite clear divine principles: He says He's against adultery, and He says He's against fornication.

The Old Testament defined *adultery* as "sexual intercourse by a man with a married woman who is not his wife." Notice that left a lot of room for married men to engage in intercourse with *unmarried* women without its being called adultery. This double standard came from the way the people regarded women—as property, not persons. That's why the Tenth Commandment says, "You shall not covet your neighbor's . . . ," and included a man's wife. She was his property.

Through the ministry of Christ and the apostles, women's position became tremendously upgraded. As women received greater freedom and status, they demanded a change in the definition of adultery. Now we see *adultery* defined as "sexual immorality between two married people who are not married to each other." But don't let this give you the idea that it gave single people the freedom to have sex. They just had another word for it. In Greek, *porne,* from which we get the word *pornography,* means "fornication," and it describes illicit sexual activity between unmarried people. The Bible doesn't act squeamish about any of this. With its straightforward standards it talks about it all and condemns it out of hand.

Alongside these standards are our contemporary mores, which take an entirely different line. Compared to the "thou shalt nots," they seem considerably more attractive, when the people who believe in them phrase their philosophies in seemingly understanding terms that sound inviting indeed. For instance those who advocate all kinds of sexual liaisons say, "Listen, we're into honesty rather than hypocrisy. We know all these people who go to church—we know what goes on behind their pious behavior. We're not like that; we're not hypocrites. We're honest." So we begin to think, *Wow, hey, that's good. Based on these mores, our contemporary society won't produce hypocrites; it will produce real, honest people.* As we begin to scratch the surface, though, we find out about that "honesty"—it's just another name for *hypocrisy!*

For instance, those who support such standards may say, "I have a meaningless relationship at home, but this one is meaningful." Now *meaningful* covers a multitude of everything, all kinds of stuff and junk. It becomes a hobbledy-gobbledy word that sounds fantastic but means nothing.

They also talk about *maturity.* "We're not going to have this backseat stuff; we want to behave as responsible adults. Instead we want to act open and mature about this. We need to look the world in the face and say, 'Hypocrites, this is meaningful, and we are responsible adults.'" Yet these "mature" people destroy spouses and children wherever they go.

Unrestrained Sexuality

Unrestrained sexuality also causes people to get into adultery. God clearly gave us a sex drive. He wanted the world populated, and He knew how to do it. Sex drive is phenomenal. But everybody knows that any healthy male could populate a small town, given the chance, so we've got to stop him. He has to have some limitations placed on him.

Well, the God who created sex drive placed the limits on it, too, but we don't want to accept them. God also invented fire, which can get out of hand. He created water, which can flood. He made all kinds of things that, unless they're guarded, may cause us trouble.

Where do we find the limits on sex today? The media glamorize and sensationalize it. Peer pressure tells us all kinds of things about it. I think we're being had.

With considerable insight C. S. Lewis said: "There are people who want to keep our sex instinct inflamed in order to make money out of it." Interesting, isn't it? He continues, "Because a man with an obsession is a man who has very little sales resistance." Think about that.

As we confront all manner of pressures about our sexuality, unless we have set solid standards, unrestrained sexuality will sooner or later overcome us, producing fornication or adultery.

Unfulfilled Desires

A lot of people today have unsatisfactory marriages. Not so long ago, to such couples, we'd say, "Tough," or even, "You made your bed, lie in it!" But in the last few years attitudes have changed considerably. If a man has an unsatisfactory marriage and can't face going home to the noisy kids, a griping wife, and a house that looks like Nagasaki just after the dropping of the atom bomb, he doesn't have to. Instead he can have a "meaningful relationship," during happy hour, over a civilized daiquiri. At a select place with cheese, wine, and hors d'oeuvres, he meets an attractive woman. *I'd be crazy to go home to that disaster area when I can have at least one quiet, relaxing hour,* he decides. It's all very innocent and understandable. He has an unsatisfactory marriage, unfulfilled desires, and unlimited opportunities. He takes those opportunities. That's how adultery happens.

What of men who reach middle age? When we hit that midlife crisis, we do all kinds of things because we want to prove we're macho men, right? No, we're really unsure about how attractive we are, whether we have what it takes. We can only find out by trying someone younger. We can't act surprised when we see women doing the same thing with younger men.

Why does adultery happen? Because people have unsatisfactory marriages and unlimited opportunities. They feel lonely, unsure, insecure, unappreciated. When they find someone who cares, appreciates them, who looks really neat, they start a "meaningful, mature relationship"—and they're on the slippery slope to disaster.

Undisciplined Life-styles

Jesus says, "If your eye offends you, pluck it out." "If your right hand offends you, cut it off." He says, "It's better to enter into life missing a limb or two than to enter hell with your body intact, isn't it?" Well, that seems like pretty powerful logic. It's also hyperbole.

Some of the early church fathers took those words seriously. One made himself a eunuch because he took Christ's words literally in his struggle with sexual desires. What Christ meant was, if you're going to avoid getting into an illicit sexual relationship, discipline your life. Don't pluck your eye out; cancel your subscription to *Playboy*. Stop putting your hand in your pocket to pay for certain channels on your cable TV. Pornography is a $2 billion business in America today. Why does it rake in so much cash? Because it has so many customers—many of them sitting in your church on a Sunday morning—simply demonstrating an undisciplined life-style.

With such an uncurbed way of life, in time, unfulfilled desires and their unrestrained sexuality, built on uncertain standards, will lead inevitably into illicit sexual relationships—in thought if not in deed.

So What Now?

I do not want to suggest that extenuating circumstances do not exist. They do. I understand the bad marriages, the loneliness, the insecurity, and all the other things that can drive a person toward that illicit romance. But I also realize that the lack of standards, undisciplined life-style, and unfulfilled desires create an explosive mix. I've picked up the pieces all over the place.

Why do we fall into such situations? Sometimes it's just because we won't call sin "sin." We substitute all sorts of polite words that make it seem less bad, so we can live with it, because we don't want to attack it head-on. Where have we gone wrong?

We can't help the sexually attractive things that go on

around us. We can't always help the stuff that bombards our ears and minds. But Martin Luther had a good word on this: "You can't stop the birds from flying over your head, but you can sure stop them from nesting in your hair." If we begin to call our lust and desire, which we've nurtured and cared for, "sin," deep in our hearts we'll begin to understand the attractiveness of this sin and avoid it.

Cure for Adultery

How do we stop adultery? We have two cures: preventative medicine and remedial medicine. If you have a choice, take my advice, and go for the preventative kind!

Preventative Medicine

How do we prevent it? First we agree with God on what He says on the subject, and we love what He says. Second, we recognize the necessity to grow in grace. Colossians 3 and Galatians 5 contrast the works of the Spirit to those of the flesh. God requires us to live in His Spirit, not on the basis of our fleshly desires. We need to agree with Him about the importance of walking with Him.

Once we have agreed with God and have begun to nurture our spiritual lives, we can develop healthy families, based on our nurturing of our loved ones' spiritual lives. This includes a healthy sexual relationship in marriage, because you can't have a healthy marriage if the sexual relationship is not strong. So agree with God on what He says. Say, "I believe. I stand on it." Build into your life a spiritual growth in grace. Put off the old things and put on your new life in Christ. Let that flow over into your marriage relationship.

Malachi 2:15 has a beautiful phrase, ". . . Guard yourself in your spirit . . . ," which describes how we can avoid sin. Once I went to a movie and a few days later got a letter from someone who had gone to see it at the same time and had walked out.

He had seen me there, and I didn't walk out; he wanted to know why. For the answer I had to sit down and search my own heart. I came up with two or three pages, a yellow legal pad long, about it.

Some people can handle certain things others can't. I look at a glass of wine, and it doesn't bother me in the least. People severely addicted to it can't even look at one. I can look at a plate of food, and if I decide that's too much, or I don't want to eat that kind, I'll say no to it. Other people can't. Things that inflame some people, so that they lose control, don't bother others at all.

What do we do in response to such situations? We guard ourselves in the Spirit. We have to know before God what we can handle and what we can't, and we have to discipline ourselves. That's preventative.

Remedial Medicine

How about remedial medicine? Our Lord Jesus was confronted in the temple one day by some pious Jews, who dragged before Him a woman caught in adultery. They tested Jesus by saying, "Moses says she should be stoned. What do You say?"

Jesus answered, "Whoever is without sin, throw the first stone." Then He began to write in the dirt, and one by one they walked out. The Lord turned to her and said, "You're forgiven. Now go away and don't do it again."

Put all that together, and you'll find some beautiful truths in this story, told in John 8. First you'll discover a loving Savior who forgives. If anyone guilty of adultery in any form repents of it, confesses, and turns from it, he or she will be forgiven; but that forgiveness cost Christ His life on the cross. It didn't come cheap. The remedial cure requires a repentant spirit, a loving Savior, and a caring community.

What about that caring community? I'll never forget the day

we opened our new church building. Ben Haden, minister of First Presbyterian Church, Chattanooga, came to give the first address from our pulpit. He took this text: "... Do not be deceived: Neither the sexually immoral nor idolaters nor adulterers nor male prostitutes nor homosexual offenders nor thieves nor the greedy nor drunkards nor slanderers nor swindlers will inherit the kingdom of God" (1 Corinthians 6:9, 10).

When I heard that text, I thought, *Ben, what on earth are you doing? You're supposed to be celebrating the opening of a new building!* But when I read the next verse, I realized what he planned to say. "And that is what some of you were. But you were washed, you were sanctified, you were justified in the name of the Lord Jesus Christ and by the Spirit of our God."

Ben went on to tell us that because we had a new building we shouldn't become too smug, because in this building we would gather forgiven sinners. That's what a church is: a community of forgiven sinners. It doesn't condone sin or condemn sinners. The church knows what we're all capable of and preaches the love and grace and forgiveness of Christ. It warmly embraces those who repent of their sins, seek His forgiveness, and live rightly before Him.

Finally, those who repent need a forgiving family. If you want to know what it means to forgive those who've engaged in this kind of sin, read the Old Testament book of Hosea. The prophet married a harlot named Gomer. A few years after the wedding, she committed adultery, and Hosea forgave her magnificently. Like Gomer, we, too, fall away from God. We need Hosea's compassion for others. Always remember that those who are forgiven much—and that's *all* believers—make great forgivers, because when we look around us, we can say, "There but for the grace of God go I."

You shall not steal.

Exodus 20:15

8

Handling Property
Properly

Not long ago I had lunch with George Gallup, of the Gallup Poll. About a thousand other people were there at the same time, but I had a chance to talk to him after his presentation, and I found out some interesting things about Christians today.

He told me that though religion has grown in popularity in our country, morality has declined. How does he know that? His organization polled the people of the United States and found out that church attendance has increased, along with Bible reading and that sort of thing. But when he did a test in conjunction with the *Wall Street Journal*, asking questions about expense accounts, income taxes, and so on, his group noticed that a high percentage did not regard cheating on these items as stealing. They thought it was perfectly all right. Even more surprising, this attitude stayed the same whether or not these people went to church. From that George Gallup concluded that many of those who claim an interest in religion do not let it affect their personal concept of morality.

Like those businessmen, many of us have a desperately inadequate view of what constitutes stealing, and we all need to take a look at what the Bible says on the subject.

The Eighth Commandment says it succinctly, "Thou shalt not steal" (KJV). In fact I understand the Hebrew really has only two words: "Not steal." Pretty straightforward, isn't it?

What shapes and sizes does stealing come in? Two. Stealing from people, and stealing from God. Let's see how we do both.

Stealing From People

In order to steal from a human being we need not merely take his money. We may deprive him of any of a number of rights by theft.

Deprivation of Property

First you may take a person's property. What does that mean? Ask a few people what property is, and you'll start an interesting discussion, because ideas about it and how you should hold it vary. We all know of the communist idea that property belongs to the state, and we understand that the capitalist says it belongs to the individual. But how many of us are aware of the biblical teachings on the subject? To sum it up quickly, the Bible clearly disagrees with both views.

Scripture certainly teaches us property is necessary and certain things should not be taken from the owner. Some of the ancient laws recorded in Deuteronomy 24 say, if you take collateral for a loan from a person, you have to be careful about what you take. You cannot take his millstone, for instance; he needs that to grind his corn and get his flour to make his bread, in order to survive. You can't take his cloak and keep it overnight, because in cold weather he would probably freeze to death without it. He needs it.

What else do we need? First Timothy 6:8 tells us we should feel content with shelter, food, and raiment. Scripture says we have the right to property in terms of those needs, and they should not be taken from us. In the Tenth Commandment, "Thou shalt not covet . . ." (KJV), we see a list of what we have the right to. But how many of us are satisfied with that list? We'd like to have blanket approval on our ownership of anything we desire. God doesn't give us that or the kind of exclusive rights we may think we have. The Bible teaches that even the property we do have rights to we hold in trust, and here's where the biblical teaching differs from that of both capitalists and communists.

Even though we need certain things and have a right to them, it's not an absolute right. Psalms 24:1 (KJV) says, "The earth is the Lord's, and the fulness thereof . . ." which simply means that everything in existence belongs to Him. That includes what you own. Your house is the Lord's. The land it sits on belongs to God. The car you drive belongs to Him. Everything you have and everything you are is His; He has privileged you with it in trust. When one person steals another's property, he not only takes something that person needs, he also takes something God entrusted to him; therefore the thief has deprived God of it and has sinned against Him. You can't really separate stealing from man and stealing from God.

Deprivation of Liberty

In order to steal, we need not take a person's property. Instead we may deprive him of liberty, his freedom to be or do. Although we most often associate such actions with totalitarian regimes, while rejoicing in the freedom we enjoy in our country, let us not forget that we, too, may deprive a person of the kind of freedom God intended him to have.

What does it mean to take a person's liberty? The Bible gives us a clue in its view of slavery—a very different one from ours. Scripture recognizes something significant when it says a slave belongs to the Lord. In other words, a person might own another one, and he might deprive that slave of liberty, but the owner still should remember that the slave belongs to God. Without owning a slave, I, too, could deprive someone else of a freedom God gave him.

In the Old Testament era, when people stole property they didn't pack up the thief and send him to jail, where he could take courses from other criminals, so he wouldn't get caught next time. Back then they had a better approach. They worked hard to ensure that people who stole could be controlled so that they could work to earn a restitution worth twice, four times, or even five times the value of what they had taken. But if a person kidnapped another, stealing that person's God-given freedom, the punishment was death. Stealing another's freedom was a serious offense.

Deprivation of Dignity

Stealing deprives another person of dignity. Everyone has a certain reputation and character. If we take someone's reputation and character from him by destroying and smearing him, we have robbed him of his due.

In Acts 19 we can see a rather interesting example of this. Paul has gone into Ephesus and has preached there. He's had a remarkable response—so much that many have turned away from the worship of Diana of the Ephesians. This hits at the trade of the silversmiths, who spend their time making ugly little silver things, shrines of Diana. The representative of the Most Honorable Order of Silversmiths of Ephesus, branch department number 217, gets upset, and Demetrius the shop steward serves up a revolt. A crowd comes into the stadium—which you can still see if you visit Ephesus today. Among other things, Demetrius complains, "These men are robbing our goddess of her majesty."

With people we can do that, too. We can take away another's majesty, his dignity, the essence of his personhood. In so doing, we've robbed him of something God invested him with.

By robbing him of justice, we may also deprive a person of his dignity. Isaiah 10:1-3 decries this with the words: "Woe to those who make unjust laws, to those who issue oppressive decrees, to deprive the poor of their rights and rob my oppressed people of justice, making widows their prey and robbing the fatherless. What will you do on the day of reckoning, when disaster comes from afar? To whom will you run for help? Where will you leave your riches?" God doesn't paint a pretty picture of the results of this kind of theft, does He?

Deprivation of Opportunity

We may steal from another by depriving him of opportunity. For example some do not understand that when they steal from their employers they have deprived them of their right to make a profit, so they don't call their acts theft. In saying that they disagree with God; the Bible talks about this in Paul's letter to Titus, when he tells Titus to teach slaves not to steal from their masters.

Now some of us may feel like slaves, but our lives hardly compare unfavorably to those of New Testament slaves. At most you may feel your company doesn't pay enough for what you do, or that they make too much profit, and because of that you may feel comfortable stealing from them. You don't call it "stealing," though; it's "ripping off." That's different!

We've developed many acceptable ways of stealing from employers today. One is calling in sick when you're not. Not only have you lied, you've stolen. But most people regard that as an absolute right. You have so many vacation days and so many sick days. You may think, *Oh, I haven't been sick, but I have the right to these sick days; therefore I will simply call in*

sick. I'll take them. In so doing, you will rob your employer of
his right: a full day's work for a full day's wage.

Maybe I don't call in sick, but I check in late or check out
early and lie about it. Or I take a longer break than I'm allowed.
Maybe I've taken home materials that don't belong to me, or
I make telephone calls I've not been given the freedom to
make.

Or we may deprive someone of opportunity by denying the
government its right to govern. The Lord Jesus made a simple,
basic statement: "Render . . . unto Caesar the things which are
Caesar's; and unto God the things that are God's" (Matthew
22:21 KJV), and people have argued about those words ever
since.

When you want a great discussion, bring up the subject of
the government. Talk about taxation. I'll guarantee that everyone who never says a word about the Bible will have a lot to
say on the subject. People have definite views on these subjects.

The Bible teaches that you pay your taxes; you don't cheat
on them. If you do, you're not "ripping off" the government,
you're stealing.

In the United States we have legitimate ways of changing the
government. If we object to taxation, we have some redress.
But as a believer, you do not have the freedom to take illegitimate means of ripping off the government, thereby denying it
what it was formed to do. You may not like the way the bu-
reaucracy spends your money, but that does not give you the
freedom to rob them of a right given to them according to the
law of the land.

Recently someone suggested that the best way to get rid of
America's deficit would be to get people to pay their back
taxes. In no time at all we'd pay off the deficit. Our economic
ills reflect our fundamental moral problem. Though we claim

to be very upright and religious, we remain guilty of stealing from both our employers and our government.

Rich and Poor

Most often when we think of stealing we think in terms of the ones who don't have, the "have-nots," taking from those who have, the "haves," what is not theirs. In the world we have a dichotomy between the haves and the have-nots. The haves have what the have-nots have not. It's a simple law of economics. The have-nots have not what the haves have.

If you're a have, you'll think it'd be great if it stayed that way. Unfortunately the have-nots won't let it stay that way, because they want what the haves have. So our natural idea of stealing says the have-nots take what the haves have.

The Bible says relatively little about this kind of theft. But it does say a lot about the haves stealing from the have-nots. "What?" you cry. "Stealing is the have-nots ripping off haves. It's mugging; it's them ripping me off; it's shoplifting. It's them doing all kinds of things like this!"

That is stealing, but so is the haves taking from the have-nots. In Deuteronomy 24:14, 15, the Bible says if you've got a poor and needy man working for you, you've got him over a barrel, because he really needs the work. He's desperate. You want to keep him over the barrel so that you can get the last drop out ofhim; therefore you don't pay him his evening wages. The law of Moses flatly forbade such actions. You had to pay a man at the end of the day; you could not owe it to him.

In other words, the Bible says you can steal from others, when you have economic control over them, if you do not give them their due when it is due. In addition Scripture teaches you can look upon suffering people and do nothing about it. When we feel we have the perfect right not to help them, we may have the freedom to feel that way, but we never got it from Scripture.

The Old Testament clearly states that the haves have an obligation to those who have not. This flies in the face of thinking of many conservative Christians in the United States of America. But Scripture teaches those who have also have a God-given responsibility to those who have not.

For example, the Old Testament says those who owned fields could not cut the corners of a field during harvest. The law allowed the poor people to come in at the end of the day and reap the corners for themselves.

In addition the harvesters could not glean after they had gone through a field. They could not go over the field at the end and rake up all the bits left in the field; they had to leave that for the poor. The Bible squarely places the responsibility for the poor people with those who have means. It insists that those who denied the needy the opportunity to survive stole from them.

Scripture most clearly describes this in the laws of the Jubilee. In the fiftieth year of a cycle, in the Old Testament times, all property reverted to its original owner. The land in Israel had been apportioned out, and the people understood that the land was the Lord's and the fullness thereof. When they received land, they held it as a trust. They could harvest it, but had to leave some for the poor.

In land ownership everybody started out on equal footing. But some were smarter than others, and some worked harder than the rest. Others were stupid and lazy. In no time flat some had more, while others had less.

In a time of calamity the wealthy might cash in on others' misfortune. As time went on the rich got richer, and the poor got poorer. God had something to say about that situation. On the fiftieth year, according to His law, all the property reverted to the original owner, which limited how rich the rich could get and how poor the poor could become. The rich had a responsibility for the poor.

When we look at this in a scriptural light, we discover stealing means a lot more than mugging or shoplifting. Whoever would have thought that in our sophisticated society we'd have to see signs on fashionable boutique walls reminding us that shoplifting is stealing? We should have known that. But for some reason we don't want to hear about it.

Stealing From God

It may surprise you that we can steal from God—and that we can do it in two ways.

Contradictory Behavior

First we can rob God of His credibility by our inconsistent behavior.

Remember when the Lord Jesus went into the temple, made a whip, drove the people out, turned the tables over, and created chaos? Among other things, that day He said, "How dare you turn this house of prayer into a den of robbers?" So some folks have said, "There you are. If you do business on church premises, you're making it into a den of robbers." When we proposed opening a bookstore at my church, I got a number of letters from people saying, "If you open that bookstore at Elmbrook Church, we will leave the church. How dare you make a house of prayer into a den of robbers?"

With all due respect to these people, I don't think they adequately understood the meaning of that story. Jesus did not mean you should never do business on the church grounds. He wanted to get across a principle the people there had missed. When they sold all the animals for sacrifice in the temple, some terribly dishonest behavior took place right before everyone's eyes. They charged outrageous prices, and anyone who brought his own animal had to exchange it for one in the temple—and had to pay even more money for an animal of equal value. The men who did this had made a spiritual profession, but their behavior ran counter to that. It wasn't a very good example of God's ways of doing things.

Today some people within the church come to us and say quite openly that they live together outside of matrimony. They're having sexual relations outside marriage and see no reason why they should stop. In doing this, they've made a house of prayer into a den of robbers, because they've robbed God of His credibility. If non-Christians come into a place of worship and see them living like that yet professing to be followers of Christ, the newcomers will say to themselves, *Those guys are phonies. This whole religion thing is a fake. Forget God.*

The best way I know of to rob God of credibility is to loudly profess one thing and live another.

Tithes and Offerings

The second way we can rob God is, as Malachi puts it, by refusing to pay the tithes and offerings. When Malachi talked to the Jews, they resisted him. They argued at every point. Finally he said, "Will a man rob God?"

They asked, "How can we rob God?"

"By refusing to pay your tithes and your offerings," he told them. (See Malachi 3:7, 8.)

Have you heard the story of the old ladies who had a new preacher in their church? The first week he preached against drinking, and they came up to him after the service and said, "That's preaching, preacher!"

The second week he spoke against running around with women. They came up to him and encouraged him, "That's preaching, preacher!"

The third week he preached against smoking, and after the message they told him, "That's preaching, preacher."

The fourth week he preached about tithes and offerings. The two women cornered him and complained, "Now you quit preaching and took to meddling!"

Some of you will think I've taken to meddling now, because as a pastor and teacher of the Word of God, I must say some of us rob God. The Old Testament teaches that if the people failed to bring their tithes and offerings to the Lord, they robbed Him.

What do we mean by a tithe? Some people have never heard of tithing; and others will say it's giving God 10 percent of your salary. But the 10 percent people have trouble deciding if that's before or after taxes.

What does the Bible teach? According to Deuteronomy 14, the people should give an annual tithe of 10 percent of all they produced to the Lord. In addition the people were to give a wide variety of offerings and sacrifices, and they also brought special thank offerings and special offerings for the building of a temple or tabernacle.

In the church we have a rare breed of people who really get into tithing, but it's not too many of us. Tithers think tithing means giving 10 percent of their income, not more. Yes, God makes that the base, but if we don't want to rob Him, we also need to learn that we hold *everything* in trust for Him. We need to get into all kinds of offerings: thank offerings, special offerings, peace offerings. That will make up a substantial part of our incomes.

Right now I can just hear someone saying, "We are not under law; we are under grace. That means we don't have to operate on that basis." I'd respond, "You are absolutely right. But wherever did you get the idea that when we come under grace we do *less* than they had to do under law? Under grace you are so full of gratitude that you take every opportunity to express it, rather than coming under a legalistic attitude that says you only have to give 10 percent."

I visited a church in Florida, where the congregation had just built a new auditorium that cost $5 or $6 million. With great glee the people told me they had moved in debt free; they had paid for it in cash before they opened the doors.

When I asked how they had done it, they told me, "Part of our membership requirement is that people tithe." Then they took me outside and showed me a three- or four-story, $11 million educational wing they had begun to build. Again they told me they'd paid cash for it. How did they do it? By tithing.

Now don't tithe just with the goal of meeting your church's budget, because budgets don't really mean that much. Tithing has a deeper purpose; it means you give to God, you don't rob from Him. When you give to God, you honor Him. You say, "Hey, God, all my money is in trust from You anyway, and I give it back to You with a glad heart." Through our giving we show we're on His side and that we have compassion for the things and people He has compassion for. We prove our love for Him by giving of ourselves.

What if we don't give our tithes and keep what belongs to Him for ourselves? That may result from an attitude of first-rate stinginess, or maybe it comes from second-rate sacrifice. Malachi told his people, "Some of you are bringing your offerings to the Lord, and you've got to bring a lamb. So you go through the flock and find one that's lame or blind, and you bring that. Do that to the governor, and see what he'd say! You wouldn't *dare* do it to him, but you don't mind doing it to God."

Strange, people feel very comfortable with first-rate stinginess and second-rate sacrifice when it comes to God. Why? Because they lack reality of the knowledge of God in their lives.

We also feel comfortable with third-rate motives. See how it works in the story of Ananias and Sapphira, recorded in Acts 5. This couple sold their land and wanted the money, but they wanted the glory, too. In the end it cost them their lives. Kind of high price tag, wasn't it?

What would happen in our churches if we took tithing really seriously and brought along all the offerings, out of our glad hearts? We wouldn't have to worry about budgets anymore. Our churches would need to hire someone just to take care of the finances and channel them into all the worthwhile projects they could find. We'd also have to find new ways to handle the blessings God would pour out into our lives.

You know why? Because God speaks through Malachi and tells us, "If you will bring the whole tithe into the storehouse, you will be able to prove Me. Get down to honoring Me, and I'll show you what I can do. And I will open the windows of heaven and pour out such a blessing you won't be able to handle it" (see Malachi 3:10). If we do that, we get the blessing; if we don't do it, we may be robbing God.

Dangers and Damages of Stealing

Various things may happen to those who engage in stealing. You don't have to look far to discover its effects, none of them beneficial!

1. It can land you in trouble with the law. Do we need to be told that? Sometimes we act as if we needed a reminder.

2. Stealing will ruin your relations with others. Do you know anyone who likes being stolen from? I don't.

3. Theft leads to deception and lies. You'd be hard put to find a thief who doesn't also lie. When someone finds out and confronts him with his actions, he will cover up.

When I had a job as a bank examiner, I became very suspicious about one man, who had not said or done anything

143

to make me think that way. At the bank they reported him as one of their best employees. In fact he never took a vacation. As soon as I heard that, I thought, *Uh-oh. A banker who won't take a vacation?* We started to look carefully at the situation and found he wouldn't take a vacation because he wouldn't trust anyone else with his responsibilities. After a month of work on the case, we discovered why. He had one set of books available for the inspectors, when they came in, and another for the customers, when they asked about their accounts. In between those figures lay thousands and thousands of embezzled dollars. The man lied through his teeth for months, denying he had done it, until we categorically proved his theft. When he knew he could no longer get away with his lies, he threw himself under a train.

4. Stealing shrivels the one who does it. His actions run counter to God's law, so they harm him morally and emotionally.

5. It places extra burdens on others. When people shoplift, the companies they steal from do not bear the cost of the lost goods; they simply pass it on to the consumer. We pay so much for our goods because we finance the thieves.

6. Stealing hinders the work of God. When Christians refuse to give to God's work generously and joyously, making it possible for that work to go on, they slow down or halt His work.

Steal No Longer

Finally, let's take a look at the blessings and bounties that accrue to us when we stop stealing. Ephesians 4:28 tells us, "He who has been stealing must steal no longer. . . ." Some people say, "I can't understand the Bible." Try that verse on them. Could anything be clearer? The whole verse reads, "He who has been stealing must steal no longer, but must work, doing something useful with his own hands, that he may have something to share with those in need."

Put all that together and you have a marvelous principle of Christian economics. If you've been stealing, come to repentance. That means admitting to God what you've done and getting into restitution—giving back or paying back the one from whom you've stolen. We desperately need restitution in our penal system today.

How can it work? W. P. Nicholson, an old Irish evangelist, preached in Belfast when that city was the major shipbuilding capital of the world. The men from the shipyards would put down their tools when the hooter sounded; they would form up and march out of the shipyards, through the streets, to the church where the dynamic speaker preached. They went straight from their tasks, in their work clothes, and filled the church. Then W. P. Nicholson would preach to them powerfully, spreading conviction, insisting on repentance and restitution. Many men accepted Christ and started to bring back everything they had stolen from the yards. In the end the authorities had to make a public announcement, "Will all those men attending the meetings of Mr. W. P. Nicholson please stop returning stolen goods. We have nowhere to store them." Imagine the unbelievable volume of stolen property that implies. Imagine the blessings!

The Blessing of Work

We need the joy of hard work, too. One of the Greek words for "work" is allied to the word for "weariness." You can get weary not doing much, but you feel somehow noble about a weariness that comes from hard work, because in the end you know you've produced something. That's what we're here for. Why? The Bible does not promise us the "good life," financially. Instead it says we should produce in order to put ourselves in the position of engaging in the blessing of giving. We need to steal no more in order to give to him that is in need.

When we come to this point we have the blessing of becoming blessings to others. In the name of Jesus we can reach out and add to His credibility—all because we've acted on this premise: "Thou shalt not steal!"

You shall not give false testimony against your neighbor.

Exodus 20:16

9

Speaking the Truth

Remember the concern God felt for His people as He told them they needed to live rightly before Him and among one another? In order to guide them, He gave them those ten handles, Ten Instructions that would show them how to love the Lord their God with all their hearts and minds and souls and strength and how to love their neighbors as themselves. The Ninth Commandment aimed at helping them show love for their neighbors.

Again we have a positive concern expressed in a negative term, to catch people's attention. The flat forbidding of giving false testimony against your neighbor expresses God's desire for His people to love the truth, examine the truth, and to live in truth and righteousness. Although we might think of this verse in terms of testimony given in a court of law, other passages of Scripture make it quite clear God by no means limits it to that. It's a good thing! We recognize our own judicial system, which says that witnesses must tell the truth, the whole truth, and nothing but the truth. We glibly repeat that phrase, but how much does it mean to us?

Look at any newspaper, and you'll find examples of our real attitudes. Edwin Moses, the great Olympic hurdler and track star, shocked the world when, not long after the 1984 games, he was charged with soliciting an undercover policewoman posing as a prostitute. The case came to court. "I didn't do it," Edwin Moses said. "He did it," the policewoman said.

In another famous trial, William Westmoreland stated that CBS libeled him when they accused him of conspiracy at the highest level of military intelligence. Their program "60 Minutes" reported that he fudged on the numbers for political reasons. He replied that he didn't. Who was right?

But these cases make us wonder. How can we know when someone tells the truth and when he lies? These men may well have told the truth, but we've seen so many other people lie and get away with it. While the court system does its best, it can't guarantee that it always makes the right decision. We've made their job harder by condoning lies, by our careless attitude toward the truth.

Today our society is in a state where people at both the highest and lowest levels seem perfectly happy saying what they want to say; and other people let them. Truth became an early casualty. Lying has turned into a way of life. In fact some circles almost encourage it, giving the impression that you just can't survive without it, and you most certainly can't get ahead unless you do it.

Against that background, let's hear the Word of God, which says you will not give false testimony against a neighbor. Proverbs 6:16-19 declares, "There are six things the Lord hates, seven that are detestable to him: haughty eyes, a lying tongue, hands that shed innocent blood, a heart that devises wicked schemes, feet that are quick to rush into evil, a false witness who pours out lies and a man who stirs up dissension among brothers." Out of those seven things, notice that two have to do with being a stranger to the truth.

Now we may dress up lying in a lot of ways. We can talk about it; we can excuse it; we can philosophize about it. I've spent some time reading philosophers about this, and it's amazing how they can muddy the waters on this subject. It doesn't take much to cover up the truth. Once Winston Churchill did not want to accuse someone of lying in the House of Parliament—that would have been a terrible thing to do. He simply avoided it by accusing that person of "perpetrating a terminological inexactitude." He meant, "You're a liar."

If we talk that way, we may end up saying, "Well, that's how it is. Nothing you can do about it." We may shrug our shoulders, like Pilate, and ask, "What is truth? It's all relative, and you really can't insist on what the Bible says."

Let's look at lying a bit more fully. Why does it seem so important to God? Why does man lie? How can we avoid it?

Why God Prohibits Lying

Lying and Satan

In John 8:43–45 the Lord Jesus makes some very powerful and scathing comments to some very religious people. Among other things, He tells them, "Why is my language not clear to you? Because you are unable to hear what I say. You belong to your father, the devil, and you want to carry out your father's desire. He was a murderer from the beginning, not holding to the truth, for there is no truth in him. When he lies, he speaks his native language, for he is a liar and the father of lies. Yet because I tell the truth, you do not believe me!"

Jesus' statement immediately puts the whole business of lying up a number of notches. He says that when we get into lying, we get into more than simply not telling the truth to somebody. He describes the devil's native language as lying. Satan doesn't know the truth, and Jesus says he reproduces people who do not know the truth—lying becomes *their* native language, too.

Involving yourself in lying means tying yourself up with the devil. Jesus has come to speak the truth, but people involved with the devil cannot even recognize it. So His words outline a massive cosmic struggle between the Father of righteousness and the father of lies. The whole universe—and all the men and women in it—gets swept up into the conflict.

Quite naturally from this we begin to understand the struggle between good and evil. The Bible says in Genesis 1 that God made everything and promptly evaluated it. He said, "It's good."

Then you read in John 10 that Jesus came into the world that we might have life and have it more abundantly. "If God made everything so good," you may feel tempted to ask, "why did Jesus need to come give us more abundant life?" The answer is that another factor came into being. John 10:10 says that the thief had come, intent on killing and stealing and destroying.

As God builds up good, Satan intently moves to destroy that good by bringing lies and untruth in the areas of truth and reality. That's why God so adamantly opposes lying and so totally supports truth: He recognizes the struggle between Himself and the devil, between good and evil, and knows that as people get swept into lies they become strangers to the truth.

A struggle also exists between truth and delusion. In 2 Corinthians 4:4 the apostle Paul talks about the devil and calls him the god of this age. He goes on to say he "has blinded the minds of unbelievers, so that they cannot see the light of the gospel of the glory of Christ. . . ." Further on he says, in contrast, "God, who said, 'Let light shine out of darkness,' made his light shine in our hearts to give us the light of knowledge of the glory of God in the face of Christ" (v. 6).

Notice the dichotomy here. Some people have minds so blinded to truth that they live a delusion. But God longs to shine into their darkness as surely as at the creation He bade the light to shine and banish physical darkness. Some people live in spiritual darkness and delusion; others have their eyes opened to spiritual truth.

Lying and Righteousness

Righteousness struggles against sin, too. God is committed to truth, to right (the Bible calls it righteousness). Sin and evil oppose Him. In our own lives we can identify when we get caught up in lying in any form. We also need to understand that we've been caught up between righteousness and sin in making that choice.

Can you understand why God takes lying so seriously?

Why Man Lies

Man has three propensities in lying, three ways of lying:

> He may lie to himself
> He may lie to God
> He may lie to his neighbor

Man Lies to Himself

One of the unique things about being a human is that you can be self-conscious or aware of yourself. In saying this, I don't mean you stand there, blushing sweetly and saying, "Aw, shucks, you know, pardon me for being here. I feel so awkward." That's only one aspect of it.

Rather I mean you have an awareness of yourself and your

actions. When I visited Kenya, I went to a game park that spreads over hundreds of square miles. In that park they have a small group of very rare white rhinoceroses—only about five of these precious animals. Because hunters prize the horns of these practically extinct animals and try to kill them, every night the game wardens lock up the rhinos, even though all the other animals range freely over the park. The men even set an armed guard over the beasts.

As we drove through the park, we decided to stop and get a look at the white rhinos. A guard came up and asked if we would like to see them. So we said, "Thank you very much. We'd like to see them—from the car."

"Oh, come out and get a closer look at them," the man invited. So we did. We walked right up to these great big things, built like tanks, munching on a snack of vegetation. One of the guards went up and patted one, and dust and gook came off the armor plating.

"Why don't *you* pat it?" he asked me. I did.

Then the guard went round to the rear end, braced himself against the rhino's feet, got ahold of the tail, and pulled it. "Now you do it." So I did. Suddenly a little voice said to me, *Stuart, that is a rhinoceros. You're pulling the tail of a rhinoceros. What are you doing?* The voice was mine. I was talking to myself. That's self-consciousness.

Part of me was conscious of me. One part of me pulled the tail of the beast. The other part said, *You're either one of the most courageous people around, or you're the biggest dummy in the area.* Got the picture?

If you begin to talk to yourself about yourself, you're self-conscious. You talk about yourself because you think about yourself. Romans 12:3 tells us we should not think about ourselves more highly than we ought to, but we should think of ourselves soberly. In other words we should use our God-given consciousness according to the truth.

If we think more highly than we ought—or more "lowly"—we lie to ourselves. We communicate untruth to ourselves. As we do that we begin to delude ourselves. We have taken the first step on the pathway to insanity: Some people so delude themselves that they no longer know the difference between up and down, black and white, or right and wrong—or reality and unreality.

When we lie to ourselves, we not infrequently perpetuate a crime against ourselves. For instance I may find myself in a situation, and I look at it. Somebody else talks to me about it and says, "Stuart, you are doing something quite wrong here." In response I immediately come up with all kinds of excuses and rationalizations. I perfectly convince myself the other guy's wrong and I'm right. When I do that, I may be lying to myself.

We see this in marriage counseling. If you try to counsel a couple heading for divorce, you try to evaluate what's going on in the marriage. As you listen to both parties you soon decide someone has to be lying. Both can't be telling the truth.

Often the person hasn't intentionally lied. He (or she) really believes the lies. Why don't the two stories agree? Because he's lied to himself. He refuses to confront reality. Instead each shucks everything off on somebody else. The root of much of man's lying to himself lies in his distaste for the harshness of the reality of himself.

Man Lies to God

To some, man lying to God may sound unthinkable. How can we possibly lie to Him?

In response to that, I'd like to take a look at Acts 5, which tells a story of the early church. Some people had great need, and others had property. The property owners sold it, brought the proceeds, and put them in the common bank, so everyone could be cared for.

One man who did this was named Joseph, a landowner from

Cyprus. He was so well-liked and well-known that the apostles gave him a new name. They called him *Barnabas*, which means "the son of encouragement." Two other people named Ananias and Sapphira watched Barnabas and thought, *We'd like to do something like that. That kind of recognition would feel good. We've got some land; we'll sell it. Then we can bring the proceeds—not all of them, just some of them—and we can pretend we gave them all.*

They did just that, but Peter saw through the whole thing. He told them, "While the property was yours, it was yours. When you sold the property and got the cash, the cash belonged to you. When you decided to give some to the church, fine. When you decided to give some to the church and pretend you gave it all, that was lying." The important thing they had to realize was, "You weren't lying to men, you were lying to God."

What led Ananias and Sapphira to do that? On the one hand they wanted to appear in favor with God, to look good to God's people. But to do things God's way would cost them, challenge them, would require decisions and change. They didn't want to go through all that. So they simply tried to capitalize on all the benefits without paying the price. When we pretend to honor Him and love Him, but won't really do it His way because it would cost us too much, we not only lie to those around us, we also fundamentally communicate untruth to God—we lie to Him.

It's bad enough lying to yourself and creating a delusion about yourself, but just imagine lying to God about yourself and ending up in a realm of spiritual delusion—a cloud-cuckoo land that doesn't reflect the real state of your faith. We find it all too easy to fall into this disastrous trap. Maybe you go to church on a Sunday and sing a powerful hymn about serving God, but if you're not careful, and if you don't mean what you sing, you could find yourself very sweetly lying to God the whole time.

Just singing a hymn you don't mean may not be a major crime, but it might signal the development of a mind-set so far removed from the reality of your heart that you will lie to both yourself and God.

Man Lies to Other Men

Finally, man tends to lie to his neighbor. Now we may do this in four ways. First through what we'll call the destructive lie— one born of malicious intent and made up of entirely erroneous content.

For example, the Sanhedrin decided Jesus was guilty and wanted the death penalty for Him. But they could not prove His guilt. Having decided all this before the trial, they got false witnesses to give evidence, so they could achieve their ends. Notice they had no interest in truth or righteousness. They decided on their goal—to destroy this man. They'd do whatever it took to accomplish that, including lying.

Not uncommonly we find such malice in our hearts—we feel a desire to destroy, hurt, or hinder someone. If we're not careful, we can go to extremes, out of that evil intent, and head toward the goal of destruction.

You remember when Joseph worked in the house of Mr. Potiphar? Mr. Potiphar went away, and Mrs. Potiphar made eyes at Joseph. When the young man wouldn't allow her to seduce him, she framed him. She felt so angry and hurt that she wanted to get even with him, so she went after him, and he finished up rotting in jail, falsely accused.

The destructive lie is not uncommon when people feel hurt and when they decide they should get even. We come across it all too often in today's society.

Next, we have the defensive lie. Peter used this after he made a great profession to the Lord Jesus, "Though all men may forsake You, yet I will not."

Jesus said, "Oh, yes, you will."

"No, no, I won't. They might, I won't."

Jesus warned him, "Before the cock crows, you will deny me three times."

"Come on," Peter told Him. "You don't know what You're talking about." Then he followed Jesus afar off. When we do that, it's always a sign of trouble.

Eventually Peter goes into the courtyard of the place where Jesus is tried, and a little girl comes up to him and says, "I've seen you somewhere before."

"No, you haven't."

"Say that again."

"No, you haven't."

"Hey, that's a Galilean accent!"

"Oh, no, it's not."

"I could have sworn it was."

"No, no, no. You're mistaken."

"I think you're one of His disciples."

"I am not." Then Peter bursts into oaths and curses, which means he begins to call on God to witness that he is not one of Christ's disciples. Lies, lies, lies, all over the place. Why? Defensive lies. He's caught and afraid of exposure. So he tries to get out of the situation by lying about it. All he manages to do is compound his culpability, to increase his guilt. It happens all the time.

Many years ago an up-and-coming young minister in the British government, married to a glamorous actress, was charged with having an affair with a call girl—not just any call girl, but one also having an affair with one of the top people at the Russian embassy. The British minister was challenged with it in front of the House of Parliament, where he categorically denied it. He lied. The next day it was proven, and the government dismissed him. That minister never again returned to political life. Everyone said that if he had admitted his wrongdoing, he could have received forgiveness. By denying it, he unnecessarily ended his career. One defensive lie destroyed him.

Then we have the defective lie, the lie of carelessness, boastfulness, silence, or half-truth. I involve myself in the careless lie when, because of a certain situation, I rather eagerly pass on information not particularly favorable to someone. I don't particularly like that person and feel more than happy to pass on the story about him. I don't bother to check it out, I just gossip about it, and out of sheer carelessness I get myself in the lying business.

Or maybe I lie out of boastfulness. Because I have a fragile ego that needs building up, I make myself out to be something I'm not. I stretch the truth, I exaggerate. I manipulate the truth so I look good—unless I'm a teenager. As William Barclay pointed out, if I'm a teenager, the last thing I want to do is make myself look good—I'd rather make myself look bad. The young girl who is a virgin doesn't want to admit that, so she brags that she isn't. The guy who wouldn't know what to do with that girl gets in the locker room and tells his friends about all the bad stuff he did with her—and he lies.

How about lies of half-truth? As a teenager I had a girl friend long before my parents would permit it. She was also four years older than I. Because of these facts, I didn't dare tell them.

When I went out in the evening, I had to explain exactly where I planned to go. I belonged to a nearby boys' club, so I said I was going there—which was true. I went to the club, walked in the front door—"Hey, hey, good to see you"—made sure everybody saw me, and darted straight out the back door. Later I came in through the back door, said, "Hey, how you doing? Good to see you," and went out the front door and home.

157

"Where have you been, Stuart?"

"Boys' club."

"Good."

Where had I been? Well, it was half true, but my intent was total deception—lying.

Now we can shrug our shoulders and say, "What is truth? It's all relative. What exactly do you mean by *lie*?" We could read philosophy to find out what other people call lying. We can discuss the thing. But I guess it's like what the Supreme Court judge said about pornography, "I may not be able to define it, but I know it when I see it." You may argue about a lie, but deep down in your heart you'll know when you've done it. Instead of discussing it, face up to the fact that lying gets us into this cosmic struggle, and that's why God opposes it.

Kind of depressing, isn't it all? How can we cure it?

The Cure for Lying

How can we combat lying? We need to take advantage of the Christian's provision for avoiding it:

> So I tell you this, and insist on it in the Lord, that you must no longer live as the Gentiles do, in the futility of their thinking. They are darkened in their understanding and separated from the life of God because of the ignorance that is in them due to the hardening of their hearts. Having lost all sensitivity, they have given themselves over to sensuality so as to indulge in every kind of impurity, with a continual lust for more.

> You, however, did not come to know Christ that way. Surely you heard of him and were taught in him in accordance with the truth that is in Jesus. You were taught, with regard to your former way of life, to put

off your old self, which is being corrupted by its deceitful desires; to be made new in the attitude of your minds; and to put on the new self, created to be like God in true righteousness and holiness.

Therefore each of you must put off falsehood and speak truthfully to his neighbor, for we are all members of one body.

Ephesians 4:17–25

This passage describes three things that come our way: learning the truth, loving the truth, and living the truth. In verse 21, "Surely you heard of him [Christ] and were taught in him in accordance with the truth that is in Jesus," we see a marked contrast to the lying and deception that go on in our world. Jesus is the truth about man, and He stands tall and true.

If we wish, we may close our eyes to Him; we can choose to give lip service to Him, yet have no fundamental interest in Him. Writing to the Ephesians, Paul says, "You have learned the truth as it is in Jesus." Have you? Have you decided that truth is found in Him, and that which is contrary to Him is by definition error? That's a monumental step to achieve.

If you take that step, you will discover the degree to which untruth and deception have become part and parcel of your life. As you begin to recognize the truth in Jesus, you then must reject the lies—the opposition to Him.

In the little town in England where I was born, we had iron and ore mines. The workers stacked up all the waste from the mines in slag banks, like mountains. Many of the little houses perched right at the bottom of the slag banks very rarely saw the light of day. Once a little lady did her laundry and hung it out in the evening. As she hung it out against the black slag banks, she felt all thrilled about how lily white it looked. She forgot the laundry, and overnight it snowed. When she went out the next morning she could not believe how yellow the laundry looked, yet it hadn't changed at all. When you hang your laundry against a black slag heap, it looks fantastic; against a white snowbank, it looks dreadful. Too much of a comparison!

Likewise, if I compare myself to my inside-out, upside-down society, when it comes to truth and illusion, I look lily white. I really need to put myself against Jesus, who is the truth, and see the truth about God, man, and life. Then I see the lies, deception, and untruth in my motives and desires, and I can come to repentance. I need to receive the living Lord Jesus, who died that my sins might be forgiven and rose again that He might impart a new power and a dynamic truth to me. The proof of the change that takes place in my heart shows in my new resolve to live in truth and righteousness.

Have you learned the truth in Jesus? Has your life taken a radical turn? Have you found yourself first confronting Him, then yielding and responding to Him?

When we learn God's truth, we start to love it. Ephesians 4:15 describes the Christian as one who speaks the truth in love. Some people try to hide the truth—and call it love. Others are so truthful they'll destroy you with it, and they call that love. Really speaking the truth in love takes a fine balance, which comes when I begin to understand how unloving it is to maliciously deceive, to delude, to destroy or defame someone. I wouldn't want to do that; I want to build them up, instead of knocking them down. I begin to love truth and hate lies.

I love truth because it is antisocial to lie. As Norman Geisler says, "Lying undermines the truth which holds mankind together." Our society requires a certain element of trust. We couldn't operate without it. If we didn't have it, imagine the financial system, the credit system! Imagine our legal system. Yet we hedge these things with rules and laws and regulations and commissions and watchdogs, and all kinds of stuff. Why? Because we know at heart we're liars.

Just imagine what would happen if all the rules, laws, and watchdogs, and the free press, and politicians were allowed to do exactly what they wanted. Scrap anything else; it's a free-for-all, and everybody can lie. After all, if you reserve the right to lie, why shouldn't everyone else have that right, too?

Take away all the restrictions and safeguards, and what do you have? A society that collapses. Because if everyone has the freedom to lie, there'll be no truth about which to lie. It's anti-social to lie; it's unloving to lie; it's also counterproductive to lie.

Ephesians 4:29, 31 tells us: "Do not let any unwholesome talk come out of your mouths, but only what is helpful for building others up according to their needs, that it may benefit those who listen.... Get rid of all bitterness, rage and anger, brawling and slander, along with every form of malice." Why? Because when you get into malice, slander, anger, rage, and bitterness, you know who you destroy first? You. Lying is counterproductive, so we love the truth. Lying also opposes the Spirit. Verse 30 directs us, "And do not grieve the Holy Spirit...." The Holy Spirit has another name, the Spirit of Truth, and anything opposed to Him in my life deeply grieves Him.

When I begin to live the truth, by exhibiting a life-style that has honesty and integrity, people begin to recognize it. But it won't be easy. Make claims to honesty, make claims to integrity, and you put yourself up to be shot at. Remember when Jimmy Carter said, "I won't lie to you"? A correspondent on the White House staff told me that as soon as the president said that, a whole group of correspondents determined to prove that he lied. They weren't interested in anything else.

It's easy to fit right into the crowd, but if you begin to say, "I stand for Christ; I stand for the truth," people will start gunning for you. But take heart, because the Bible says, "Blessed are those who are persecuted because of righteousness." Today we desperately need men and women who will begin to live the truth. When we live the truth, we can begin to talk it. Once we have shown it in our actions, we can start to proclaim it with a degree of credibility. You'd be hard put to sound convincing, if you tried to communicate the truth in Jesus and everybody had already proved you a liar. Who would listen to you?

The Ninth Commandment says some powerful things to us in those few words, "Thou shalt not bear false witness against thy neighbour" (KJV). The New Testament puts the same principle positively when it tells us, "Therefore each of you must put off falsehood and speak truthfully to his neighbor, for we are all members of one body.... Do not let any unwholesome talk come out of your mouths, but only what is helpful for building others up according to their needs, that it may benefit those who listen. And do not grieve the Holy Spirit of God ... Get rid of all bitterness, rage and anger, brawling and slander, along with every form of malice. Be kind and compassionate to one another, forgiving each other, just as in Christ God forgave you" (Ephesians 4:25, 29–32).

We need to discover those truths for ourselves daily, turning from the lies that bind us, to new freedom in Christ.

*You shall not covet your neighbor's house.
You shall not covet your neighbor's wife, or
his manservant or maidservant, his ox or
donkey, or anything that belongs to your
neighbor.*

Exodus 20:17

10

Forbidden Fruit

In the last Commandment, we have something different from
the rest, because while the first nine deal with actions, the last
addresses our attitudes. Accordingly we find it much easier to
talk about the first ones, because we don't have a hard time
identifying actions. We can see and verify them, while an attitude may remain hidden.

Why would God spend all that time on action rules, then
suddenly throw one in on attitudes? If we take a good look at
that final one, we'll discover that to a real extent covetousness
pervades and prevails in many of the first nine forbidden activities. This last Commandment kind of ties in all of them, when
it talks about how the law relates to what lies inside our hearts.

Where Does It Come From?

The word the Hebrews got *covetousness* from has the same
root as the word meaning "desire" or "delight." If you think

about it a little, you'll latch on to the link between the two ideas. Seeing covetousness as an inordinate desire for something that may very well be delightful makes a lot of sense. After all, who would covet something that held no attraction at all for him? He sees it, likes it, and begins to tell himself he has to have it—he covets.

Does that mean we should have no desires and delight in nothing? No. God initially gave us the desires and filled the world with delightful things for us to enjoy. Having given them, however, He warns us, "Now don't desire delightful things wrongly." That statement clearly confronts us with the problems of identifying those wrong desires and admitting to ourselves how we have mishandled delightful things. We need to find the right balance, because along with giving us the desires and delightful things, God has also denied us certain things. If we ignore what God has set off limits, simply allowing our desires to go unfettered, we find ourselves in covetousness.

God-Given Desires

God has given us a number of good desires that we may pervert from His purpose by our attitudes. First, He has clearly given us the desire to acquire. In itself nothing is wrong with that. He gave squirrels a desire to hoard nuts for the fall, and it's a good thing He did, because otherwise they would never survive winter. He gave birds a desire to collect straw, mud, and feathers to build a nest; and if He hadn't, they wouldn't have a place to lay their eggs and raise their progeny. By the same token He gives us a basic desire to acquire things. Our God-given survival instincts are clearly related to this acquisitiveness.

He also gives us the desire to succeed. We can see the influence that has on us in the common fear of failing. If we didn't feel so afraid, we would attempt to do more than we do. But we try to avoid the downer of failure because we have a built-in expectation and desire for success. Presumably God put us in this world to achieve something, to be something. We want to do those things, but we see no merit in failing at what He wants. So we avoid anything that might not end in success.

We have a God-given desire to produce. When He created mankind, God made it clear that He expected man to take the raw materials with which He had filled the world and to use them for the glory of God and the benefit of man. Anyone who fails to do so lives below his God-given humanity and the desire to progress that He gives. We all should enjoy that tremendous drive to discover more, to bring more and more of the divine creation into subjection in order to derive benefits from it.

God-Given Things

God has given us delightful things, too. He made the world, put man and woman in it, and they looked around and called it "pleasant." When God saw His creation He said, "That's good." They were delightful pieces of work. God's into the delightful business; He doesn't make anything shoddy. He filled our world with good things.

Truth is delightful. In Psalms 19:10 the Bible says we should desire His precepts, that God's truth is delightful, more precious than gold, and something about it enraptures our soul. To us He has given the exciting ability to know truth. God has taken the initiative to reveal truth to us, and He says we can find it in His Word. As we work the silver mine of God's Word, enjoying a delightful exploring process, instead of being confused about life, we find ourselves locked into the truth.

The apostle Paul says we should desire (or in the old translations *covet*) gifts because God has given us delightful, desirable gifts. He has filled our lives with them. Of course Paul speaks specifically about spiritual gifts, in this passage in 1 Corinthians, but He has also given us much more.

So you put this all together, and what conclusion do you come to? That God has filled creation with love and truth and all manner of delightful gifts. In addition, He has given us desires.

Covetousness means our God-given desires have gone wrong. We may simply describe it as greed, and in actual fact some desires may easily move into greed. Or we may call it lusting after beautiful things, but that ignores the fact that God made them beautiful. We need to think carefully about what we would include here.

God has given us certain denials along with those desires and gifts. He has said, "So far and no further!" He has told us "This person [or that thing] is off limits." What does He deny us? Four things.

Desiring Excessively

God does not prohibit us from desiring, but He does deny us the right to desire excessively. If we do that, we have gotten into covetousness.

But what is excessive? If you start working it out, you'll discover one person's excess describes another's normal experience. If we don't think carefully, we may characterize as need what God calls greed. We have to respond to Him with sensitivity. For if we move out of the area of genuine satisfaction into the insistence of naked greed, we tread on forbidden areas.

Read the Old Testament prophets, and you will find that they continually complained to God's people that the covenant people had become consumed by greed. Over and over God makes it clear that one of the reasons the Hebrews went off into captivity was their covetousness. They desired far more than they needed and thereby demonstrated how covetousness had consumed them.

Desiring Illegitimately

Second, God denies us the right to desire illegitimately, despite the fact that we may see delightsome things and want them. For some things God says, "No entry. Keep out. No way. Forbidden territory." He's made it abundantly clear.

Remember the story in the beginning of Genesis that tells how God put man and woman in the world, demonstrated His love for them, and only wanted their love in return? But you can't make someone love you. You can't grab ahold of him, by the hair, and say, "Fall in love with me." You can only have love when a person makes that free choice.

If you can only love by choice, you have to allow the person the ability to choose. So God gives man options. He fills the whole area with delightful things, and in the middle puts a fence around one thing, saying, DON'T TOUCH! If Adam and Eve chose to obey, they would demonstrate their love. If they disobeyed, they would show their rank disdain for God. Maybe the tree God fenced in was no more beautiful than the others. The man and woman certainly had more trees in the garden than they could handle. Only one was forbidden territory, forbidden fruit.

What happened? Of course those two went right ahead, climbed over the fence, grabbed the stuff off that forbidden tree, and demonstrated disdain for God.

Now God has done that all along the line. On some things He puts up a NO TRESPASSING sign. He moves into certain areas of our lives, and says, "This is a delightful thing. You have desires that respond to that thing, but don't touch, because to do that would be illegitimate." We can simply thumb our noses to God and say, "Get lost, Lord!" But if you see a delightful thing

God has placed off limits and hold back, you demonstrate your love for Him.

When we insist on desiring the illegitimate want, we fall into covetousness and insult God. Joshua 7 clearly illustrates this with the story of Achan. When the children of Israel came into the Promised Land, God forbade them to take plunder. Achan saw a bar of gold, silver, and some beautiful clothes and took them. The Israelites went into battle and got roundly defeated. Immediately God told Joshua of the sin in the camp, and they worked by process of elimination until they confronted Achan. What did he confess to when he came forth? Covetousness.

Desiring Exploitatively

If we desire things at the expense of someone else, we exploit that person for our benefit. God speaks against this very powerfully indeed in 2 Peter 2:3 "In their greed these teachers will exploit you with stories they have made up. Their condemnation has long been hanging over them, and their destruction has not been sleeping."

The Tenth Commandment illustrates what God expects by prohibiting others from coveting a neighbor's house, wife, maidservant, manservant, his ox or ass, and then God says—in case He hasn't said it clearly enough—nor anything that is your neighbor's. What does that mean? If you see your neighbor's possessions and think he's doing nicely, and you say, "I want what he's got," and you set out to get it, you will exploit him for personal advantage. That is the essence of covetousness.

How easily we do that in our society, which builds so much on competition and the survival of the fittest and where we go after it and get it, because we do a better job than the other guy. How quickly our desires begin to exploit others!

Desiring Exclusively

God also denies us the right to desire exclusively, to just want more and more things. In Luke 12 we read of a time when Jesus spoke to the people, and one of the crowd said, "Teacher, tell my brother to divide the inheritance with me." Jesus replied, "Man, who appointed me a judge or an arbiter between you?" Then He said, "Watch out! Be on your guard against all kinds of greed; a man's life does not consist in the abundance of his possessions." Our society flatly repudiates the Golden Rule and Christ's teachings on this point. Instead it tells us, "We have the inalienable right to pursue happiness," and the clear implication is that we find happiness in possessions. In the original draft of the Declaration of Independence, Thomas Jefferson wrote that man had the inalienable rights of life, liberty, and the pursuit of possessions. The committee that worked on the document changed the wording, but our thinking hasn't changed at all. We all feel our happiness lies much with our things. Jesus says, "No, it doesn't." We answer, "Yes, it does." Here modern North American society and Jesus meet head to head. "Watch out," says Jesus. "Be on your guard against all kinds of greed, because if you think you have the inalienable right to happiness, and if you link your happiness with your possessions, then to be more happy you will want more possessions, and that's covetousness."

He goes on to illustrate what He means when He talks about a certain rich farmer, who did very well, got a bumper crop, and didn't know where to put it all. He would simply expand, he decided: Pull down his old barns, which were obsolete anyway, and build bigger, better ones. He thought, *You have done a good job. You have plenty of good things laid up for many years. Now take life easy. Eat, drink, and be merry.* That farmer sat back and voted himself a roaring success, but God gave him an F. *"Fool,"* He said. "This very night your life will be demanded from you. Then who will get what you have prepared for yourself?" (Luke 12:20). That's what happens to anyone who stores up things for himself, but is not rich toward God.

In writing to Timothy, Paul said we bring nothing into the world, and it is clear we will take nothing out. What do you do between the nothing you start with and the nothing you end with? If you get absorbed with a lot of things, you have simply moved from nothing to things and back to nothing. We need another standard of measurement. Jesus put it this way, "Lay up for yourselves treasure in heaven, where moth and rust do not corrupt and where thieves do not break through and steal" (see Matthew 6:20).

If I get greedy, I get caught up with things, and what happens to eternal issues? What happens to the spiritual elements of life? If I live with things all my life and forget God, I'll end up a nothing. That's why God denies us the right to desire exclusively.

Remember He gave us the desires and made the delightful things. But He built in the denials, too. Covetousness means worshiping desire, committing my life to the fulfilling of my wants. I do it when I pursue one delightful thing after another and reserve the right to them without any restrictions.

What Does Covetousness Do?

First, covetousness leads to dishonesty and injustice. David saw Bathsheba. He lusted after her; he coveted her. Clearly he understood the Tenth Commandment. But she looked delightful. David was all man and had God-given desires. Although he knew God had put her off limits, he denied the denial and committed adultery. End of story? No, the beginning. That opened a sad chapter of dishonesty, injustice, and one disaster after another in his life.

In our society today, when we go for all the gusto we can get, ignoring God's denial, we open up much hurt and pain in our lives. We can see the results on every hand.

Let's face it, we confront many beautiful people, and a lot of us don't have entirely satisfactory marriages. We don't feel satisfied, because we're reading what sex should be in *Playboy*. If our partners don't measure up to that standard, we'll find all kinds of problems and delightful alternatives to them. As we move off into all kinds of exotic ways to enjoy ourselves, we may have fun and excitement, but we may also wreck people's lives. Let's call covetousness what it is: sin that leads to all manner of destruction.

Look at Ahab, Jezebel and Naboth. Naboth had a little vineyard, a piece of the family territory that God had given him. King Ahab got all the territory around it and wanted that vineyard. He went to Naboth and said, "Hey, listen, I want your vineyard. Just let me have it, and I'll pay you and give you some other territory."

Naboth replied, "I can't do that. This is God-given land that belongs to my family. It's been ours for generations, and it has to stay there. Even if it went away, it would have to be returned to me at the Jubilee; you understand that, Ahab."

Ahab went away and sulked, but his wife, Jezebel, didn't like her hubby sulking. So she said, "What's the matter?"

"I can't have Naboth's vineyard," the king pouted.

"Don't worry about that. I'll fix it."

She fixed it all right. She lusted after the vineyard and went after it for her husband. Jezebel put Naboth up in the public place and brought forth witnesses against him. They charged him with unspeakable things, and by law they put him to death.

"Great, get your vineyard, husband," the queen announced.

Simple covetousness led to injustice, which led to betrayal, which led to all kinds of unspeakable things. In other places the Hebrew word translated "covetousness" means "to cut off." Cut off easily leads us to "rip off." That's what covetousness will do—rip off all kinds of people.

Creates Insatiable Demands

Covetousness creates insatiable demands. In Mark 7, Jesus described it this way, "Look, Pharisees," He said. "Don't think what you put into your body corrupts it. That's not what does it; it's what comes out of your body that's corrupt." He listed a whole lot of stuff that comes out, including covetousness. "It's there, it's within us," He warned. We all share that built-in, natural tendency to covet.

If we accept that, do we also accept the fact that our society lies in dire danger? One of the Greek words for *covet* means "to have more"—just more and more and more. In recent years we have worshiped at the shrine of an expanding economy. We want everybody to have a job. That's a noble goal. If everyone has a job, we'll have increased production. The more we produce, the more we have to sell. If we want to sell more and more things, it means people have to buy more and more. So we work to persuade people to buy more.

How on earth can we do that? Well, some smart business people know the theory of Mark 7, even if they've never read it in the Bible. They know everybody has a tendency toward covetousness. So our expanding economy learns to manipulate the consumer.

Now we've gotten into a vicious circle, because if we cut back, we finish up with more and more people out of work. They become more and more of a burden on society, have less and less income, pay less and less in taxes, and we've entered a nasty economic downward spiral. At the root of the whole problem, we have our tendency toward self-interest, which leads us into covetousness, because our society and economic principles almost demand it. Chances are, we don't even realize what's happening.

In his book *Wealth of Nations* Adam Smith, writing in 1776, said, "Man's basic most important motivating force in all economic matters is the drive of self-interest." In other words, "What's in it for me?"

You want something more up-to-date? George F. Will wrote in 1984: "The most familiar and fashionable variety of conservativism is strangely soothing. It tends complaisantly to define the public good as whatever results from the unfettered pursuit of private ends."

He points out the flaw in our thinking when we assume that national good can come out of everybody having the freedom to pursue their own selfish ends. If he's right—and I think our economy proves he is—we're sitting on a powder keg. On the one hand our economy says, "More, more, more. Produce more, sell more, get more." On the other hand God warns us, "Don't covet. Your greed will kill you." Are we sensitive to this weakness in the spirit of our age?

Confuses Moral Judgment

Ephesians 5 tells us the pursuit of personal gain can become an idol. We get so caught up in improving our lot, making our self-interests that which dominate our lives, that if we're not careful, we worship at the idol of self-interest, in the shrine of personal gain. When that happens, we've confused our moral judgment by our covetousness.

What happened to the man in Luke 12, who wanted eternal life? Jesus told him to get rid of his possessions, come back, and follow Him. That young man answered, "No way." The Lord

Jesus made it clear that this wealthy fellow deified material things—that was where his heart was. Jesus said, "Where your treasure is, there your heart will be also." If your treasure's here on earth, that's where your heart will be. If your treasure is stored up in heaven, your treasures down here will be relatively insignificant. When we get this wrong, we often don't even realize it.

How Can We Respond?

When we have it all backwards, we find ourselves worshiping ourselves at the expense of others. All that matters is what we get and what we want, getting what we desire, doing what we want to do, and going where we want to go. What can we do to combat it? First we have to take what God says seriously. When it comes to coveting, He says, "Don't." We need to search our hearts and ask some questions. *Am I greedy for position, prestige, praise, or possessions? Is my ego so fragile that I need more and more possessions to make me happy? More praise to make me feel good about myself? Am I hungry for more prestige, greedy to be recognized by more and more people? Do I need a secure position that no one will challenge? Do I constantly reach for these things?*

We need to search our hearts, to ask ourselves if self-interest primarily motivates us. Do we use the words *I, me,* and *mine* too often? Do we frequently think only of ourselves? Does the world seem to revolve around us? Have our lives begun to show the influence of "Dallas" and "Dynasty" life-styles?

If we spend much time with such things and little with the Word of God, we probably are riddled with covetousness and don't even realize it. If we see our covetousness, we need to confess that sin, saying, "This is where I moved into forbidden territory." Then we have to adjust our life-styles. We can easily talk about searching our hearts and confessing sin, but we need to take some action in our lives, too. That's the problem.

What happened in the course of pursuing all those things? Did you do so in order to share them and make them available to others? We may give our tithes, and as we succeed in the things of this world that money grows and grows, but boy, that other 90 percent gets bigger, too, and we spend it in extravagant life-styles.

What does it mean to limit our life-styles? We look at the way we live and say, "This far and no farther." We do not need that house or the expensive vacation. We do not have to purchase another new car. We avoid status-symbol buying and unnecessary spending. Instead, as God gives us more and more, we discover, to our delight, that we have more and more to give. We have more to share.

We find it hard to call covetousness sin, repent, and turn from it. Because they don't exist, I can't offer you any simple solutions. But remember what Scripture says, "Godliness with contentment is great gain." All of us want contentment, but we've swallowed the lie that the more we have, the more contented we'll feel. Really the more we have, the more worried we become about keeping it. The more we have, the more we want.

To cure this, we have to put a lid on it, and we have to see expansion as an opportunity to give as unto the Lord. If I love money, I overlook the fact that the love of money is the root of all evil. I'd better get back to feeling satisfied with food and clothing. Why? Because the writer of Hebrews says we can be content because the Lord is our portion. If we want to live as if we really believed that, we'll have to make some radical changes in our lives.

Will it be worth it?

You can count on it!

11

Meeting the Commands' Demands

When God brought His chosen people out of Egypt, He established a covenant with them. He would be their God, and they would be His people. With them He wanted to work in all the nations around them, demonstrating what it meant to have a relationship with Him. The Israelites would love the Lord their God with all their heart and mind and soul and strength; they would love their neighbor as themselves. Those actions would show they were His unique people.

To give them practical help in showing God was number one in their lives, He gave them four Commandments. To help them know how to love their neighbors, He gave them six more.

Keeping the Commandments

Today, thousands of years after the giving of those Commandments, to what extent do we have to keep them? How do we meet the demands of the Commandments? What should they mean to us?

No One Righteous

In Romans 3:20, Paul says, "Therefore no one will be declared righteous in his [that is, God's] sight by observing the law; rather, through the law we become conscious of sin." That verse makes two very important statements about the Ten Commandments. First it says that no one will ever be right with God because he or she has fulfilled the Ten Commandments. That comes as a surprise to some people.

You'll come across many folks who will tell you, "I live by the Ten Commandments." They'll say it with a smile of satisfaction on their faces. The fact that they can't even recite the Commandments doesn't bother them at all. They don't know them, but they live by them. "It's my code of ethics, and that's enough," they'll tell you.

Some people, particularly those brought up in areas with a profound religious influence, feel that if you give such a half-hearted attempt at keeping the Commandments, you're okay. God thinks you're a good guy and feels just delighted to have you on His side. But that's wrong thinking. Scripture declares quite categorically, "No one will be declared righteous in God's sight by observing the law." Why? Because no one has ever done it. Paul describes the law this way, "The law is holy, it is righteous, it is good, and it is spiritual." But then he goes on to say, "Those of us who would be justified—declared righteous by fulfilling the law—have got to remember something. We're required to continue in *all* the law to do it. We are not allowed to approach the Ten Commandments with selective indifference."

Have you noticed how we tend to pick and choose among the Commandments? If we're really into the decline of our society, we notice the one that says, "Thou shalt not commit adultery." We get after all those adulterers around the place and attack those who think adulterous thoughts. We really come down hard on all those sinners!

But the fact that God said, "Thou shalt not covet" rolls off us like water off a duck's back. It's all right to be greedy, as long as you don't commit adultery, isn't it? You can lust after property, wealth, or position, as long as you don't lust after your neighbor's wife.

We don't have the freedom to have such attitudes. If we want to keep the Ten Commandments, we have to keep all of them, and I have yet to meet the person who can go down the whole ten and say that he's kept them all.

One young man who met Jesus thought he had kept them. The Lord Jesus listened with great interest as he told of his perfections. He responded, "Well done, young man. There's only one thing you need to do now. Go away, sell off all your property, and give it away. That's all you need to do. Then come back and be My disciple." When he heard that, the young man gagged on the words and went away sad. Why? Because he approached the Ten Commandments with selective indifference. He wanted to get rid of number ten. It said, "Thou shalt not covet," and he was riddled with covetousness. Jesus put His finger on the spot.

If we want to keep the Commandments, we can never slip up. Sometimes we have spiritual high points, and we feel all enthusiastic. We see a TV program or go to a conference or go to church and get all pumped up. Then we begin to run out of gas. As we leave the meeting or stop watching TV we hear a "hiss-s-s." Soon we can see the sag it causes in our spiritual lives. If we want the Ten Commandments to justify us, we can't have high points and low points. We can't only feel interest in them spasmodically. We have to keep all ten, externally and internally, all the time.

Conscious of Sin

Romans 3:20 also tells us the second thing we need to learn from the Commandments. "No one will be declared righteous in his sight by observing the law; rather, through the law we become conscious of sin."

Perhaps we feel rather pleased with ourselves in thinking

we're rather nice people. We're probably right. Our mothers taught us the social graces, how to behave, and we can cover up certain things. We know how to get along with people. Maybe we've even learned how to make friends and influence people. But what are we when we aren't performing? How are we when we're alone? We need to know ourselves as we really are. The Bible says the law helps us do that.

Some time ago, when Jill and I visited the Ivory Coast, we went to a school for missionary children. One day at that school, some children were playing around the base of a tree and found a hole in which they saw something beautiful indeed. They had a wonderful time looking and chattering about it, until one of the teachers noticed what they were up to. He investigated and immediately said, "Kids, get away from that." He herded them off and rushed to get three or four African workers.

One of the men climbed down into the hole, while the others held on to him. Then this beautiful thing lying in the hole suddenly struck, grabbed onto the man's leg, and began squeezing it. They held onto the man, it held onto the leg, and they pulled both of them out and with a machete chopped off the head of the twenty-five-foot-long python. I saw the skin hanging on one of the dormitory walls, when I visited.

Like those children, we can look at the hole under the tree and play with something that seems gorgeous, until a situation brings out its true nature. Do you know what you really are on the inside? To find out, apply the law of God.

"What shall we say, then?" Paul asks. "Is the law sin? Certainly not! Indeed I would not have known what sin was except through the law. For I would not have known what it was to covet if the law had not said, 'Do not covet.' But sin, seizing the opportunity afforded by the commandment, produced in me every kind of covetous desire...." What is Paul saying in this passage in Romans 7:7, 8? He tells us that within each of us lies the latent capacity for sin. Somehow we have to come to terms with our sinful capacity. A lot of us don't believe it's there, so something must be applied so that sin will reveal itself to us. The sin coils itself up, nice and beautiful, inside us, and on the outside we're lovely people. Somehow or other God has to make it strike, so we can know it for what it is.

The Ten Commandments make it strike. As we expose ourselves to them we discover how greedy we are; we discover how lustful we are; we discover how much we can become strangers to the truth, when it serves us. As we look at these and the other sins it has opened our eyes to, we ask, "Is that me?" The answer is, "Yes. That's the *real* me."

Nobody will keep the law, and we have to recognize our own sinfulness through the law, as God applies it to our lives.

Made Right With God

In Romans 8:3 we read, "What the law was powerless to do in that it was weakened by the sinful nature, God did...." What was the law powerless to do? It could not make us right with God. The Ten Commandments cannot make anyone fit for heaven and cannot equip us to live as we ought. Why? Because of the weakness of our sinful nature.

Now this does not mean there is something wrong with the law. It means there's something wrong with the material the law has to work with. Many years ago, when I went to high school, we had a teacher who came in to do choral music in our school. He had a tremendous reputation for producing marvelous choirs all around the area. Yet he left our school in utter despair. Why? Because there he found a bunch of kids who didn't like music or who didn't want to sing, even if they did like music, and every single one had a voice like a cinder under a door. It was just bad news.

Now that's not to suggest our teacher was not a brilliant musician—he was. The material he had to work with caused the problem. The same is true of the Ten Commandments. They have to work with me and you. We have a sinful nature that remains apathetic toward God's law or is antagonistic toward it. Because of our nature and the holiness of God, we don't have what it takes when it comes to fulfilling the Ten Commandments.

Listen to the good news. What the law was powerless to do, God did. What did He do? He sent His Son, in the likeness of sinful man, to help man know God. And Jesus fulfilled the law. He was the Ten Commandments on two legs, living, breathing, warm, and magnificent. Now added to the law that condemns us, we have the life of Christ to condemn us. But Jesus didn't just come to do that. He went to the cross as a sin offering. All the consequences of the broken law, all the curse upon us for not being what we should, all the consequences of our sin nature coming to the fore and striking against the law and doing all manner of things wrong—God heaped those up, gathered them together, and placed them on Christ, who died for our sins.

Have you ever met anyone for whom Christ did not die? Have you met someone for whom His death did not blot out sin, cleansing him and making him right with God? The answer is no. Because that person has not been born and will not be born. We are the very people for whom Christ died, that we might be forgiven.

A Change of Heart

Maybe you want to ask, "Hey, if the Ten Commandments are no good, why bother studying them?" I'm glad you asked. There's one final thing about the law.

The Ten Commandments are important to us because, when

they show us our sin, lead us, ashamed, to Christ, so that we might be forgiven, we can come alive through the Lord Jesus Christ, who died for each of us. What does He do when He comes into my life? He writes His law on my heart. That means He changes my desires and my aspirations. He alters the direction of my life and gives me the power to change. As the living Christ comes into my life the righteousness of the law becomes fulfilled in me. First I find a new love for the Lord. I desire to have Him first. I have a new interest in the Lord's day and a new concern for others. As I see lust and greed for what they are, I turn from them. All those things that are sin begin to move away.

Because of the changes in my heart, I begin to demonstrate I'm walking in the law and fulfilling the righteousness of the law.

Once, on a plane, I had my Bible out, doing some catch-up reading. A stewardess came up and said, "Mustn't spill coffee on the good book, must we?"

"No, we mustn't," I responded.

A while after another one had a word with me, then stayed, and we talked. She said, "You know, four years ago the Bible was a dead book to me. Then something happened, and I can't explain it, but I can't get enough of it. I devour it."

"I know what happened," I answered. "Have you ever read a book that was boring, then one day you met the author? Afterwards you picked up the same book and said, 'I know who wrote this,' and it became the most exciting book in the world to you."

"Yes, that's what happened to me. I met the author."

When you meet the author of the Word of God, He begins to write it in your heart instead of hitting you over the head with it. You begin to desire it instead of resenting it. You long to see it work out in your life, rather than saying, "Why does God say this to me?"

That change of heart shows you've repented of your sin, God has forgiven you, and that the living Christ has come into your heart. Now the law of righteousness is fulfilled in you, because you walk after the Spirit, not after the flesh. As you go through life you increasingly become the Ten Commandments on two legs, living, breathing, moving, warm, demonstrating your love for the Lord and your love for other people. It becomes important to you.

As you've read have you gone through the Commandments saying to yourself, *Heh-eh, I kept that one.* Or did you say, *Yeah, I'm all right on this one,* only to discover later, *Uh-oh, he got me!* Did you notice that bit by bit you found different things you'd kind of slipped up on? Well that wasn't the point.

The point *is* that as we expose ourselves to the law and keep it—which we haven't done—we begin to understand that by it no one will be made righteous. In addition we start to discover the sinfulness of our own sinful nature. Does that bother you? Did you begin to say, *O God, what on earth can I do?*

God says, "Nothing. I've done it. I've given Christ as a sin offering for you. Now you know your sin, you know the impossibility of getting rid of it, but listen up. I have taken your sin and placed it on Christ. He died for you. If you will come to Him and acknowledge what you are and ask Him to forgive you and invite Him to come and change your heart, your mind, and your life, He will."

How far have you gotten with all that? As you look at your life, can you say, "That's what I was and this is what I am?" Can you say, "The law showed me my sin and led me to Christ. I was forgiven. The living Christ came into my life by His Spirit and changed me. Now I have an overriding desire to live His way?" If so, you'll know you're different.

If that hasn't happened, it sure needs to, because if it doesn't, your sporadic efforts at keeping the law will no more fit you for earth than they will help you into heaven. Here your feeble efforts will seem pretty useless, while they won't do a thing at all to right things with God. Only God can change your spirit, when you come to Him in repentance. Halfhearted efforts to keep the Commandments won't open the way to eternal life.

Where are you today? Do you need to make a first commitment to God? If the answer's yes, why not take time to do so now? Or do you have a commitment to Him that has gotten a bit fuzzy or frayed around the edges? Use this chance to review what God has done for you. Spend some time with Him in prayer and get things straightened out.

Then take time out to learn what it means to play by the rules!

Suggested Reading

Anderson, Norman. *Issues of Life and Death.* Downers Grove, Ill.: InterVarsity Press, 1977.

Barclay, William. *The Ten Commandments for Today.* New York: Harper & Row, 1983.

Bernbaum, John A., ed. *Perspectives on Peacemaking.* Ventura, Calif.: Regal Books, 1984.

Carson, D. A. *From Sabbath to Lord's Day.* Grand Rapids, Mich.: Zondervan Pub. House, 1982.

Catherwood, Frederick. *First Things First.* Downers Grove, Ill.: InterVarsity Press, 1979.

Clouse, Robert G., ed. *War.* Downers Grove, Ill.: InterVarsity Press, 1981.

Davidman, Joy. *Smoke on the Mountain.* Philadelphia, Penn.: Westminster Press, 1953.

Gardner, R. F. R. *Abortion.* Exeter: Paternoster Press, 1972.

Geisler, Norman L. *Ethics: Alternatives and Issues.* Grand Rapids, Mich.: Zondervan Pub. House, 1971.

Goudzwaard, Bob. *Idols of Our Time.* Downers Grove, Ill.: InterVarsity Press, 1984.

Kaye, Bruce and Gordon Wenham, eds. *Law, Morality and the Bible.* Downers Grove, Ill.: InterVarsity Press, 1978.

Mackay, Donald M. *Human Science and Human Dignity.* Downers Grove, Ill.: InterVarsity Press, 1979.

Palmer, Earl F. *Old Law—New Life*. Nashville, Tenn.: Abingdon Press, 1984.

Schlossberg, Herbert. *Idols for Destruction*. Nashville, Tenn.: Thomas Nelson, 1982.

Watson, Thomas. *The Ten Commandments*. Edinburgh: Banner of Truth Trust, 1965.